Stories Behind Record Fish

Stories Behind Record Fish

Complete Angler's Library™
North American Fishing Club
Minneapolis, Minnesota

Stories Behind Record Fish

Library of Congress Catalog Card Number 91-62283
ISBN 0-914697-41-2

Printed in U.S.A.
1 2 3 4 5 6 7 8 9

The North American Fishing Club
offers a line of hats for fishermen.
For information, write:
    North American Fishing Club
    P.O. Box 3403
    Minnetonka, MN 55343

Contents

Acknowledgments

The North American Fishing Club would like to thank everyone who helped make this book become a reality.

This book would not be possible without the cooperation of the many record holders who contributed their stories, the staffs of the International Game Fish Association and the National Fresh Water Fishing Hall of Fame, and the outdoor writers and fish and game officials who helped the author find many of the record holders.

Wildlife artist Virgil Beck created the cover art. Photo contributors included: Alaska Department of Fish & Game, American Museum of Natural History, Atlantic Salmon Association, Bill Baab, George Baab, Allen Benas, Jim DeOtis, Edward B. Elliot, Ted Furnish, Dan Kadota, Coke McKenzie, Penn Reels, Pradco: Rebel Lures, Tom Rosenberger, Gary Studdard, Charles Taylor, Russel Tinsley and Dr. Robert White.

A special thanks to the Fishing Club's publication staff for all their efforts: Editor & Publisher Mark LaBarbera, Managing Editor Steve Pennaz, Managing Editor of Books Ron Larsen, Editorial Assistant Colleen Ferguson and Art Director Dean Peters. Thanks also to Vice President of Product Marketing Mike Vail, Marketing Manager Cal Franklin and Marketing Project Coordinator Laura Resnik.

1

About The Author

Louis Bignami would be the first to tell you he helped eat several line class record bull trout last year in Idaho after he went home to check the record book and a helpful neighbor filleted their fish for smoking. Or that he lost a fly rod tippet class striper record when a plug caster on the other bank snagged his line. One time when he was going to star in a fishing video, the camera crew couldn't find the boat in the fog and his wife caught the only fish of the day. So he says, "I guess it looks like the only way I can get into a record book is to write it!"

Louis started fishing in the California Sierras for trout when he was a child in diapers. As a youngster, he caught jack smelt in San Francisco Bay and carp on dough balls in Golden Gate Park. Since then, he has caught roosterfish in Mexico, bonefish in Florida, tarpon in Costa Rica, salmon in British Columbia and billfish in Hawaii. He was a licensed guide in California, specializing in trout, salmon and steelhead trips and seminars.

Louis resides in Idaho. He says, "I live about halfway between the 20-pound steelhead in the Clearwater River and the 20-pound landlocked salmon in Coeur d'Alene Lake, so I can fish anytime the pups don't look too pathetic and force me to shoot birds."

His early careers included field archaeology, banking, professional tennis, the U.S. Army and real estate manage-

ment. After graduating from college and law school, and working as a bank trust officer, Louis started writing upon discovering that "nobody happy has any reason to see a lawyer." He has sold several thousand articles and photographs; he has authored, or co-authored (with his wife, Annette) nearly a dozen books.

Louis is a member of the Outdoor Writers Association of America, Society of Professional Journalists, American Society of Journalists and Authors, and Idaho Director of the Northwest Outdoor Writers Association. He has won OWAA awards for his writing.

Louis has been trying to catch a 10-pound bonefish for 30 years. His wife caught one her first time out in the Bahamas, but told the guide to release it, because she "didn't want to fill the space on the wall that Louis has saved for so long."

Dedication

To my wife, Annette, who besides being my best friend, true love and disgustingly lucky when we fish together, stands for all the fishing widows that get too little credit.

She represents the wives that take the photos fishermen and outdoor writers claim. She started with the wives that handle the home and hearth, while husbands fish. She learned to fish, shoot and photograph, and became a member of the Outdoor Writer's Association of America.

Today she's a member of the larger group of wives that go along and suffer the same privations, but get too little applause. So, this book is for Annette, a loving lady who managed to survive 15 years home full-time in the writing game, an economic blood sport not for the weak who whine or complain.

Foreword

L ike most NAFC members, I like to page through the list of
world angling records and dream about the day that I catch
a record fish. Of course, I know the odds are against me. The
largemouth record has already stood more than 50 years
(though it is getting shakier every year), and I have yet to see a
15-pound walleye, let alone a 25-pounder. Still, the dream is
alive, especially after returning from the first-ever NAFC
Adventure of a Lifetime to Rio Colorado Lodge in Costa Rica.

Six of us made the trip. Joining North American Fisherman
Editor & Publisher Mark LaBarbera and myself were NAFC
Charter members Morris (Moe) Mendel of Cleveland, Ohio;
Dick Stoesser of Midland, Michigan; and the husband-and-wife
team of Don Foster and Becky Embree of Moberly, Missouri.

The fishing was slow the first morning for everyone but Dick
and Moe who braved rough seas beyond the rivermouth. They
jumped 11 tarpon before lunch, losing two to sharks and
landing one. In contrast, Mark and I went without a hit. Don's
and Becky's luck was about the same.

After lunch, Mark and I headed out to the surf with a very
reluctant guide, while Moe, Dick and their guide followed in
their boat. Ceasar, our guide, stopped just beyond the

rivermouth and instructed us to cast toward shore. I protested when Dick and Moe continued past us to the spot where they had hooked all the tarpon earlier, but Ceasar was convinced we would find good fishing where we were.

For the next hour, Mark and I worked the entire shoreline but failed to take a fish. Then, almost imperceptibly, something nudged my Rapala. I set the hook instantly, but missed. With renewed interest, I continued to work the area. Four casts later something nudged the Rapala again. I set the hook hard.

Instead of jumping, the fish took off on a short, powerful run. I knew it wasn't a tarpon, so I turned to Ceasar and gave him a "What is it?" look.

"Jack crevalle," he guessed.

Disappointed, I continued to work the heavy fish. Fifteen minutes later Ceasar grabbed the heavy mono leader and lifted, his gaff poised and ready. Suddenly, he tensed up and yelled, "Big snook, big snook!" just as the fish took off on its final run.

The snook was too spent to go far, however, and I was able to lead it back to the boat within a minute. Ceasar slipped the gaff under the gillplate and lifted. He had trouble bringing it into the boat.

I was stunned when I saw how big the fish was. Held at eye level, the mighty snook stretched well below our guide's knees. I knew it was a possible line class world record.

"Let's get this fish on the scale while it's still fresh," I told Ceasar. He was already pulling up the anchor.

The rust spring scale back at the dock registered an even 30 pounds, which surprised me because the fish looked much heavier. A quick check of the International Game Fish Association (IGFA) record listing showed the 16-pound line class record at the time was a 34-pound, 8-ounce fish. Close, but no cigar.

At the urging of the chef, we left the fish on the scale so he could prepare it for dinner that evening, and headed back out for the rest of the afternoon.

Don and Becky were waiting for us when we returned to camp that night. They had jumped four tarpon that afternoon, but were unable to land any.

We were unloading the boat when I noticed something peculiar about the scale—the needle was resting a full seven pounds under zero! My snook, the one we were having for dinner that night, was a probable line class world record.

That night, I realized that setting a world record involves both luck and skill, though not necessarily in equal amounts. As you read through the exciting stories behind the record catches, you'll notice some records are earned with minimum luck and years of preparation, while others involved incredible amounts of luck. The end result is the same, however.

If you're interested in setting a world record, read through the rules in the appendix of this book and contact both the IGFA and the National Fresh Water Fishing Hall of Fame and ask them for an application blank and their latest record listings including line class fly-rod records. Setting a world record for many species is easier than you might think. In fact, it's probable—if you're willing to fish for some of the less popular species.

Enjoy *Stories Behind Record Fish*.

Steve Pennaz
Executive Director
North American Fishing Club

The Mystique
Of
Fish Records

1

Going After Records

Izaak Walton understood records when he said, "No man can lose what he never had." Nobody *has* a record, you just hold it until you pass it on. Some fishermen don't understand this. They feel records offer special virtue or status. Records seem to reflect man's desire to order his world. Records, aside from the cash value some species hold, seem to be in conflict with Walton's concept that "I have laid aside business and gone fishing." Records also conflict with his perceptive statement: "Doubt not but angling will prove to be so pleasant that it will prove to be, like virtue, a reward in itself." Hemingway had a solid handle on the situation when he noted that "only the first catch counted, for every other record may be broken."

Since it's man's nature to make lists, rank achievements and compete, we have had fishing records since cave men drew Atlantic salmon on the wall. Today, two major groups, the International Game Fish Association (IGFA), and the National Fresh Water Fishing Hall of Fame (NFWFHF) keep records. Where listings overlap—IGFA lists women's records, but has a smaller number of line classes; NFWFHF adds ice fishing and other listings—they can disagree.

However, it's not the numbers, lists and records that count. It's the record that is a shorthand report of someone's achievement that seems most important. The journey, if you like, not the destination, remains the real story that we will tell here. So these efforts large and small may inspire you to seek your own record, and realize that, if only records bring happiness, there are more losers than winners.

Given the number of record possibilities and the number of open line classes, it's possible for anyone to set a record. It's even likely. Some records are lucky. Others reflect a long, often expensive quest. Most records represent an opportunity seized by a fisherman with enough skills to get the job done with, of course, considerable luck. Readers can make up their own minds about the degree of each in the accounts that follow.

All-Tackle Records

All-tackle records are the big ticket hits on fishing's Wheel of Fortune. Perry's largemouth bass record, if broken today, could be worth $1,000,000 to a lucky and skilled fisherman. Glassell's black marlin saltwater version isn't worth as much in endorsements, although you can be sure that millions have been spent in its quest. Big boat billfishing isn't for the budget-minded!

Line Class Records

Line class records can reflect more skill than all-tackle attempts. Catch a fish five, 10 or even 20 times the line test—the record is Kelley Everette's pacific blue marlin that weighed 37 times his 30-pound line's test. Other line class records are silly—a 2-pound fish on 50-pound test, for example. These records demand close attention to rules and current standards; it's possible to lose a potential record with line that's too light, as well as that which is too heavy!

Fly Rod Tippet Class Records

Fly rod all-tackle and tippet classes are other areas where skilled anglers who know the regulations use them to their advantage. There seems considerable argument about existing tippet construction requirements, add-on butts and other gear used to improve the angler's chances.

Women's Records

Even though women's saltwater records are still kept separate from men's in the IGFA, women, proportionately to

This giant sea bass, all 454 pounds of it, earned for Lillian Scott the IGFA women's 50-pound-test record. It was taken after a three-and-a-half-hour battle.

Going After Records

their numbers, take more big fish than some chauvinists like to admit. Women traditionally show best in lighter line classes. For example, Mrs. Marian Hasler, with famous guide Tommy Gifford, caught the first tuna over 350 pounds taken on 15-thread line—"thread," the designation in days of woven line, ran 3 pounds each. So 15 thread would be 45-pound test. Mrs. Hasler also landed a world-record, 530-pound broadbill on 24 thread and a 246-pound swordfish on 9 thread. In these days of women's equality, one wonders how much longer these classes will last even in the conservative IGFA.

Luck And Records

Some records are earned with minimum luck and maximum preparation and angler output. DeOtis' lake sturgeon, Glassell's black marlin, Marron's swordfish, Everette's Pacific blue marlin and a number of others seem to relate more to sheer effort than good fortune. The typical record is a mix of luck and enough skill to do the job as you will see in the salmon, blue catfish, brown trout, redear sunfish and bluegill chapters.

Just plain luck helps. The near 100-pound flathead catfish record, taken on a No. 4 hook while crappie fishing qualifies here. So does either the IGFA or NFWFHF black bullhead records, Torres' near record largemouth bass and Lettie Robinson's black crappie.

Some fishermen have no luck. The Greater Miami Fishing Tournament even has a hard luck trophy for this kind of situation. It's named for Phillip Wylie, a famous unlucky fisherman and writer. The first year it was offered, the award went to Jim Scully, a fisherman who wanted an IGFA record more than anything else in the world. After years of trying, he finally caught a world-record amberjack. In less than an hour, his fishing companion, Bart Harborn, caught an amberjack that weighed 5½ pounds more. Harborn wasn't even interested in records, but his catch meant Jim Scully lost his record.

The Oldest Record

Some records are so old that you would think nobody would care. Ande lines listed Dr. C. C. Abbot's 4-pound, 3-ounce yellow perch as one of their records in a recent press release, but this looks doubtful. The record was set in May 1865, and monofilament wasn't even a concept until just before World War II. There might seem to be other doubts about this antique record, too. Homer Circle, who ran national fishing contests for years, said, "The biggest yellow perch I saw during 20 years ran between 2 and 3 pounds."

The site of Abbott's catch, Crosswicks Creek, which is a tributary of the Delaware River, suggests that the fish might have been a freshwater drum some call "sheepshead."

Other listed perch records also seem to support these claims. The largest line class NFWFHF perch was a 2-pound, 3-ounce specimen taken by Steve Stopich ice fishing on Little Bay du Noc in Michigan in 1984. IGFA lists three perch between 2 pounds, 5 ounces and 2 pounds, 1 ounce, all caught by Ray Johnson as part of his record-setting blitz during Berkley's Trilene record reward program. So, with no proof and scanty records, Dr. Abbot's perch would seem as doubtful as a cure for the common cold. Still, the white perch record at 4 pounds, 12 ounces is also considerably larger than the next ranked fish of its species.

However, according to Ben Callaway, a well-known outdoor writer who lives in Cherry Hill, New Jersey, you must consider the source.

"Dr. Charles Conrad Abbot was one of New Jersey's most ardent naturalists," Callaway said. "He lived on a plantation-like farm in Hamilton Township (between Trenton and Bordentown), which is now built up to a heavily-populated suburban area.

"He roamed the state to record specimens or to observe phenomena concerned with all fields of natural history. He was an author in natural history and ornithology.

"He was also an ardent angler and took the record perch from Crosswicks Creek which runs a few miles in back of his farm. It seems most doubtful that Dr. Abbot would misidentify as conspicuous a fish as a yellow perch, and, aside from the curiosity value, he would have no reason to do so."

Callaway concludes, "I couldn't get anything else on that yellow perch, but it is accepted by everyone I know, even the most cynical types."

So it seems likely the record is correct as a skilled naturalist would hardly mistake one species of fish for another. However, see black bullhead and black crappie chapters!

Setting Your Own Record

A record starts with enough research to find a line class or, in limited cases, an all-tackle record that is within reach. "Fish where the big ones bite" remains solid advice so check existing records. Membership in the IGFA and, for freshwater fishermen or those who want to see lots of open line classes, the NFWFHF is a must. Their annual record listings insure you don't, as Mike Leech at IGFA says happens every week, call up after the fact and discover you just ate a record fish.

Planning for the catch comes next. The location of the nearest certified scales, or, if you fish in remote areas, having your own scales properly certified, is a must. DeOtis had to drive for miles when he noticed the scales he planned to use hadn't been certified within a year as IGFA requires. Torres may have lost a world record by waiting hours before his fish was weighed. McKenzie had to put up with over 40 years of "second best" interviews about his bluegill, because he waited overnight to weigh it. So, the message seems clear—get the big fish weighed as quickly as possible or you may regret it.

Record Rigging

Rigging for records requires close attention to IGFA regulations, and some knowledge of the more liberal NFWFHF approach. IGFA limited line classes, strict requirements for terminal tackle—no trebles with bait, for example—and a realistic approach to the use of double lines and long leaders established as a result of their initial saltwater orientation.

Both organizations require line samples for testing. It's important to realize that the "test" on 6-pound test may really be 8 pounds. At least one line salesman offered "the strongest 10-pound test line on today's market." He was right, it broke at 16-pound test. So, to be safe, buy line that's rated to IGFA specifications.

Realize, too, that you can find weak spots on some NFWFHF line classes at higher tests. Thus, you might want to make sure such line tests high. Paul Kadota, for example, lost a line class record on black bass when his line tested too low. So did Marlin Coulombe.

Bill Riesenfeld, fishing out of Key West, Florida, became a world record holder in the IGFA men's 4-pound-test category with this 44-pound, 2-ounce permit. His guide, Joe Wejebe, held it for the picture.

IGFA Regulations

The IGFA publishes detailed regulations in their annual that also lists all-tackle and line class fresh- and saltwater records, fly rod records and the top three fish in each class taken that year. The following are highlights and potential problem areas within the IGFA regulations in meeting requirements for IGFA records.

Line Regulations

Equipment regulations prohibit the use of wire line. If backing test is higher than the main line, the higher test shall apply. Double lines are allowed and measured from the knot to leader. (Double lines and leaders should always be measured a bit short so that, as the line stretches during a fight, it still falls under the association's maximum, allowable lengths.)

Double Lines And Leaders

Double lines and leaders combat abrasion from the fish or snags. Their use is critical for lighter line classes, and always important. In saltwater classes up to and including 20-pound-test double line must be at or under 15 feet and the combination of double line and leader not to exceed 20 feet. All classes over 20-pound test are limited to 20 feet of double line with the combination not to exceed 40 feet.

Saltwater leader length includes the lure and the like with no limits on the strength or material of the leader. In up to 20-pound-test line classes, the leader is limited to 15 feet. Over 20-pound line classes, the limit is 30 feet with combinations as above. Freshwater double line sections can't exceed 6 feet; leader sections can't exceed 6 feet. The combination of double line and leader can't exceed 10 feet.

Rod & Reel Regulations

Rods must comply with sporting ethics and customs. Tips must be a minimum of 40 inches in length, butts can't exceed 27 inches in length, except for surf rods. (A 4-foot long ultra-light might not have a 40-inch tip, but would probably qualify anyway—ask!) Powered reels, ratchet handles or two-handed cranking reels, like sailor's winches, aren't allowed.

Hooks And Lures

IGFA does not allow double or treble hooks for bait—this cost a record in the brown trout line class. Hooks must be embedded in the bait to eliminate snagging. Other regulations apply, and applications must include photos or a sketch of the bait's hook arrangement.

Lures are limited to two single hooks with skirted lures and may not trail hooks more than a hook's length behind the skirt. Plugs can have up to three sets of single, double or treble hooks. Photos or sketches of terminal rigs are required.

Incidental Gear

Offshore addicts should note restrictions on fighting chairs and gimbals. Gaffs and nets must not be over 8 feet in overall length, and flying gaffs not more than 30 feet. The flying gaff restriction came in after a pilgrim hooked a giant jewfish, couldn't move it from its lair in shallow water, and dove over the side of the boat with a gaff on a rope to hook and haul in the fish. Rules also prohibit lances, harpoons or floats, except for small bobbers to float bait.

Overall Regulations

Only the fisherman will hook, fight and, except for gaffers or netters, touch the fish, the line or the gear. If the rod is in a holder, the fisherman, not a second party, must grab the rod and start to fight the fish. There is a stated, if often ignored on shallow flats, intent that fish be played off the single, rather than doubled line. Harnesses and such are attached to the fisherman, not the boat. All laws and equipment regulations shall apply.

IGFA has a list of disqualifying acts that include second parties touching the rod, reel, angler or double line during the fight; resting the rod on a holder or gunwale of the boat while playing fish; handlining fish; changing rod or reel while fighting fish; intentional foul hooking; breaking a rod during the fight and others. Many of these regulations apply more to saltwater conditions than to freshwater, but IGFA takes a very dim view of violations and carefully checks witnesses and paperwork.

All-Tackle And Line Class Regulations

An all-tackle record fish also holds one line-test record. Line classes run 2, 4, 8, 12, 16, 20, 30, 50, 80 and 130 pounds, with sensible upper line-test limits on some species—20-pound test on largemouth bass, for example. How would you like to catch a huge bass flippin' with 25-pound test and have it disqualified? Several large sharks have been disqualified for the use of lines over 130-pound test.

Record Weights And Weighing

Records must be a minimum of a pound in weight and must either outweigh the existing record, or meet minimum weight requirements. If fish weigh less than 25 pounds, new records must be at least 2 ounces over the old record. Records over 25 pounds must be a minimum of .5 percent over the old record.

Otherwise, a tie results. Weighing must be done by an official weighmaster, IGFA official or recognized local person familiar with the scale. Witnesses are recommended. The tackle used must be displayed to the witnesses and weighmaster. Fish must be weighed on dry land; no estimated weights are allowed. Scales used should be certified within the past 12 months, or recertified as soon as possible after the catch. (Anglers can use their own scales in remote areas if other scales aren't available and their scales are certified.) IGFA recommends that anglers serious about records carry a copy of its record book and application form, as well as a camera, film and tape measure. It also helps to know the location of certified scales in advance.

Deadlines

Anglers must submit an IGFA application form, length of line and terminal tackle and acceptable photographs that include side views of the fish, the tackle and scale used and the angler with the fish within 60 days if it is caught in U.S. continental waters, and within 90 days for other waters. The exception is well-documented all-tackle records from the past.

NFWFHF Regulations

The National Fresh Water Fishing Hall of Fame takes a more liberal attitude toward records than the IGFA. They offer more line classes, a wider assortment of permissible line weights for most fish, and alternative records for ice fishing, "no reel" classes and the like. While the NFWFHF lists mostly U.S. records, it also lists records and species from Europe. Like IGFA, they prohibit powered reels. Their minimum rod length is 26 inches, handlines aren't allowed, and they require the first 25 feet or more of line for line class testing. How this can be done and also satisfy IGFA requirements for dual record certification is open to question. In most cases, fishermen seem to send the first 25 feet to IGFA and the next to NFWFHF. This can produce records in different line classes for the same fish. Regulations are rather relaxed. No mention is made of double line. Baits and lures aren't restricted and, if the method is legal in a state, it will usually work for NFWFHF. Photos are also required and the time limitation overall is 90 days with "exceptions allowed for good cause."

Cheating

You can't mention records without dealing with cheating. Fishermen have cheated in fishing contests at least as far back as the time Anthony and Cleopatra bet on a fishing contest held on her royal barge. The historian Plutarch notes that Mark Anthony hired a diver to put a "great fish" on his hook. Cleopatra, the next day, hired another diver to put a salted stockfish on his hook. Numerous cheating stories exist. Fishermen have stuffed their catch with lead—the more subtle use baitfish. One lodge was famous for sending its fishermen out with plastic bags. When a possible record fish was caught, it was stuffed in the bag and the lodge certified the weight of the fish along with disgorged bait and water. Another rumor claims a record holder weighed in a fish that his wife actually reeled in part way. Surf-caught record fish have supposedly been purchased from commercial fishermen; it goes on and on. Rumors are worth little without proof.

If you define cheating as "rule breaking" then it's clear that those who shoot halibut or sharks won't meet IGFA rules. If you define cheating as "breaking the law" then you might have to include fish that are snagged or taken off floating jugs legal in Texas and a number of other states. Vermont, for example, has a short season when you can chase pike into shallow water and stun them with gunfire. Many states allow bowfishing for rough species. Some allow floating jugs, trotlines with multiple hooks or as many outfits as an angler can afford. Perhaps the best rule on an individual basis is "fair chase."

Fair Chase

The IGFA and NFWFHF regulations and state laws only offer minimum standards. No rule prevents fishermen from unfair advantage. For example, trolling for a billfish with large baits and quickly backing down on fish so the mate can grab the leader, upsets some. Fly fishermen grouse about multiplying reels and, while using bobbers—described in the literature as "strike indicators"—and nymphs as large as ultra-light plugs, complain about bait fishermen or spincasters. Casters claim trollers take unfair advantage with electronics. One state banned depthfinders for a time. Many fishermen no longer cast over nesting bass.

Some, who swallow the light tackle hook, play fish for such a long time that lactic acid builds up and, even when returned to the water, fish die. A recent German ruling is rather interesting. Their court claimed "catch and release" is inhumane, although fishing for food was allowable. Clearly, "fair chase" doesn't depend on legal or record prohibitions. It's your ethical decision. Someone once described ethics as, even when unobserved, "behaving as if a favorite aunt with a very large estate, was watching." "Fair chase" is just that; it's based on respect for the fish as much as concern for the record.

Trophy Taxidermy

If you are lucky enough to catch a record or even a respectable fish, you might consider releasing it to breed. You no longer need to keep a trophy fish to have a mount for the wall. Fiberglass mold technology and some quality air brush work from a good photo of your fish create all "glass" mounts that don't deteriorate and, unlike skin mounts, stand up to changing temperatures, areas where people smoke and inevitable wear and tear.

If you insist on a skin mount, you still need a quality color photo taken from the side with fins extended. Try to do this in open shade to avoid glare that hides important details.

Next, kill the fish humanely—a trophy has survived long enough to deserve that. Most recommend a sharp knife inserted through the gill covers and spine after the fish is weighed—see IGFA regulations. Don't puncture the fish's skin or gut it. If, because of an extreme boondock situation, you must gut the fish, slit it horizontally halfway up the side that will go against the wall when the fish is mounted. A minimum-size cut is best.

Wrap the fish in a wet towel and put the package in a big plastic bag. Put the bag on ice—a freezer is best, but a cooler works. Once the fish is frozen you can take the time to contact a quality taxidermist and get prices. However, the lowest price at a local taxidermist who "usually does birds" may not insure a quality, lasting mount.

Many experts recommend taking several good photos, keeping the fish in the water, measuring the length and girth, releasing the fish and getting a lasting fiberglass mount.

Freshwater Records

2

$1,000,000 Bass?

Bob Kutz, director of the National Freshwater Fishing Hall of Fame, says, "The next world-record largemouth bass, if it ever comes, will be worth a million dollars. Prizes, endorsements, outdoor shows; it could be incredible." Stu Tinney, then publisher of *Striper* magazine, once noted, "A million? I could make more than that the first year. If you could keep the bass alive, there's no telling how much you could make." Times do change. George Perry caught his fish on a shared rod and reel that cost $1.33 with a $1.35 lure. This was used with some 25-pound-test waterproof silk line from a row boat built from 75 cents worth of second-hand lumber scraps. It was 1932. The depression raged. Perry took his fish home and ate it. His bass was so big it took his family two days to finish eating the fish.

The Perry Record

In interviews before his 1974 death in a plane crash, Perry said, "We were out to catch dinner. We only had one lure, so we shared the rod and the rowing. When it was my turn I tossed the lure back into a pocket between two fallen trees and gave the plug a couple of jerks.

"All at once, the water splashed everywhere! I do remember striking, then raring back and trying to reel. But nothing budged. I thought I'd lost the fish—that it had dived and hung me up. What had me really worried was the lure, it was the only one we had between us."

As Perry remembered it, the fight wasn't much. It rarely is with really huge bass. After the fish was landed, Perry toted it over to the J. J. Hall and Co. General store. In a *Sports Afield* article Perry said, "It was almost an accident that I had it (the fish) weighed and recorded." A buddy mentioned the *Field & Stream* contest with its $75 merchandise prize. So Perry took his fish to the post office where, several hours after it was caught, the big female weighed 22 pounds, 4 ounces and measured 31 inches long and 27 inches around.

"It created a lot of attention that day in Helena," Perry said. "The old fellow in the general store weighed it. He was also a notary public and made the whole thing official."

Perry's family remembers the story a bit differently. According to George Baab's report in the February, 1989 *Bassin'*, "Someone at the store mentioned the (*Field & Stream*) big fish contest and urged daddy to enter it. He had the fish weighed on a set of certified scales at the post office. According to the contest rules, he had the fish's dimensions and weight notarized. The fish weighed 22 pounds, 4 ounces.

"Then, Perry took his fish home and his mother, Laura, fried one side for supper, along with onions and tomatoes from the garden. They ate the other fillet later. Nobody took a photo, but the family does have a replica of the record bass and the lure Perry used."

There does seem to have been much confusion about the lure. According to Baab's article—he is the top authority on Perry and other bass record holders—"The lure was a Wiggle Fish in perch scale manufactured by the Creek Chub Bait Co." For a time, few could agree on the lure's identity. It was variously identified as a Fantail Shiner, Jointed Wag-Tail, Creek Chub Minnow, Creek Chub Wiggler and Creek Chub Wiggle Fish. Baab discovered a letter from the son of one of Creek Chub Co. co-founders that, on the basis of conversations with George Perry, identified the lure as a No. 241 jointed perch Wiggle Fish. Even today the makers of the line, rod and reel used by Perry remain unknown.

Perry, except for his name, remained relatively unknown, too. He never seemed very impressed with his record. This shouldn't be a surprise. Perry, according to George Baab, then

Members of George Perry's family, including his widow, Pauline (third from left), hold the replica of his world record largemouth bass. The replica includes the same type of Creek Chub Wiggle Fish lure the record fish hit on.

outdoor editor of *The Augusta Chronicle*, "was a quiet, modest, but confident man."

In 1932, when Perry caught his big bass, he was a poor young man of 20 whose father had died the year before. Perry had to help support his five brothers and sisters. With only an eighth-grade education, and barely literate, he educated himself and worked his way up to owning Perry's Flying Service at the local airport. He eventually died in an air crash.

Naturally, he won the *Field & Stream* contest with his 22-pound fish. He took his $75 prize out in a Browning automatic shotgun, a rod and reel, shotgun shells and some outdoor clothing. Prices have gone up! At the time, this seemed to Perry like all the gear in the world. Then, just to show his first fish was not entirely an accident, he won the *Field*

& Stream contest again in 1934 with a 13-pound, 14-ounce largemouth.

Today, there is a commemorative marker next to Georgia Route 117 just two and one-half miles from Montgomery Lake, a side channel wide spot in the Ocmulgee River near Perry's home in Helena, Georgia. Perry might not have understood that. Like most brought up in the depression, he knew the difference between the necessary—shelter, family, food and job—and the merely nice, like record fish. He did understand the changing economics of recreation. In 1973, when interviewed by Baab just before his death, he mentioned that the record, if caught then, might be worth $10,000. Today, the record is clearly worth 100 times that. Even so, his daughter said, "If daddy had been a different sort of person, he could have made a pile of money doing public speaking about his record." Another friend, Dr. William F. Austin of nearby Brunswick, said, "George was never very impressed by the fish, or interested in impressing anyone about it."

The Lost Record

Most bass fishermen know, and many lust after, the Perry record. Very few ever wondered about the record Perry broke. Bill Baab did wonder. While the old *Field & Stream* records—from days before IGFA and NFWFHF handled this chore—had been destroyed, Baab turned up a 20-pound, 10-ounce largemouth. It was caught by Fritz Friebel who had held the record for nine years prior to Perry's fish. It reportedly came from Moody Lake in the Florida panhandle. Friebel's brother claimed the fish came from nearby Big Fish Lake, though. This record is listed by Florida, but is considered "uncertified" under the sunshine state's new, tough rules.

In any case, Friebel, a traveling hardware salesman who always toted fishing gear, fished Sunday morning in May of 1923 with a couple of friends. Friebel took his fish with a Creek Chub Straight Pikie Minnow. It measured 31 inches long with a 27-inch girth. The girth might have been off. Friebel's daughter, in a later interview, said, "A fellow accused Daddy of loading his fish with lead sinkers. So daddy cut the fish open and let the fellow feel inside." Like the Perrys, the family ate the fish soon after.

Raccoon Fish, Weight Eating Bass And "Maybe" Records

When Baab researched bass records, he discovered an account in an Indiana newspaper of a 24-pound, 12-ounce fish caught from Lake Tohopekaliga near Orlando, Florida, in April of 1974. This suggests Disney World visitors who skip the fishing might be missing out!

Raymond Tomer reportedly caught the fish on a dark plastic worm. His fishing partner and two witnesses testified to the weight, and that it measured 39½ inches long and 30 inches around. Tomer put the fish in the cooler, but the cooler lid wouldn't shut. So when he filleted the fish to cook it, it had spoiled. So he threw it out. He did nail the head on a post, but raccoons ate the head that night. Without the fish, its head and supportive photos, Florida Game and Fresh Water Fish Commission, and others, refused to recognize the record.

Another large, and controversial bass, was caught by Sandra DeFresco in Miramar Lake, a southern California impoundment. When first weighed, it created a lot of excitement. Later, after a 2½-pound diver's weight was removed from its belly, the bass still weighed in at 19 pounds, 1 ounce. NFWFHF recognizes the fish at its "post-weight" weight as the 15-pound line test record. It's not recognized by IGFA. As Mike Leech of IGFA remembers, "We had a problem with the 2½-pound diver's weight. Also, if I remember correctly, the lady who caught the fish had the rod break and handlined it. That's also grounds for disqualification."

Torres' Big One

Leo Torres had no clue about records when he went fishing at Lake Castaic in early 1991. His story even now seems a bit vague. One report said he used lead-core line, another that he used 12-pound-test Trilene XT. When interviewed, he had to reflect for some time before he could remember the Mitchell reel and Shakespeare rod he used.

All accounts agree that he caught a big fish on bait. How big? When measured, it ran 30¼ inches long and its girth was 27 inches. Twelve hours after being caught, it weighed 20.96 pounds. It's possible the fish could have topped Perry's record. It seems certain that its measurements and, "fresh weight" ran larger than the second place fish at the time.

Mike Arujo poses proudly with his latest major catch, a Lake Castaic largemouth that, at 21 pounds, 12 ounces, had just become the California state record. It was just seven ounces short of tying the all-tackle world record.

Crupi-Arujo-Kadota California Challenge

A trio of very serious bass fishermen who fish southern California's Lake Castaic often and well seem to present the most serious challenge to Perry's longstanding record. Their efforts in early 1991 fell just ounces short of retiring Perry's name from the record books.

On March 12, Bob Crupi, a Los Angeles-area policeman who lives on Castaic, caught a giant, 22.01-pound female while fishing a point with live crayfish. Crupi's catch came just one week after another dedicated Castaic angler, Mike Arujo, had taken a 21.74-pound lunker with a 6-inch rainbow trout-pattern Renosky Super Shad from the same reservoir. Both catches eclipsed the California state record of 21 pounds, 3 ounces, set in 1980.

However, Arujo's fish is the official state record because Crupi released his catch without having a California Department of Fish and Game fisheries biologist verify the catch. Arujo's catch which he kept was inspected. Both catches had been sufficiently documented to be submitted to IGFA as line-class records. Crupi already holds the IGFA's 12-pound line class record and NFWFHF's 10-pound record with a 21-pounder that he caught in Castaic in March 1990. Crupi's

Dan Kadota took a mighty run in 1989 at breaking George Perry's record as he took a 19-pound largemouth from Lake Castaic in California in January and came back in December to take these two—a 15.26-pounder and a "baby" 12.93-pounder.

22-pounder would replace his 12-pound record while Arujo's catch would raise significantly the 16-pound line class record from the 14-pound, 3-ounce fish that previously held that record.

California's denial of Crupi's bid for a state record set off a controversy concerning the state's promotion of catch-and-release. Critics maintained that if Crupi had kept the fish so that a DNR official could inspect it, then the fish probably would have died. Critics claimed the inspection provision was a contradiction of the state's promotion of catch-and-release conservation.

Crupi, for his part, had his 1990 catch mounted, and decided to return this fish to the lake because he felt "there was no need to kill a world-class fish that could produce world-class off-spring." Besides, with another year's foraging on Castaic's riches, including threadfin shad, Mississippi silversides, crayfish and stocked rainbow trout, this female could easily be the world record bass.

Dan Kadota holds the IGFA 20-pound line class record with a 19-pound largemouth taken from Castaic in 1989. But he's pulled a number of 18- and 19-pounders from the lake, and is considered a good bet to break the record. Kadota devoted most

$1,000,000 Bass?

of his early fishing career to saltwater as captain of a charter boat. He approaches bass fishing in Lake Castaic with the same devotion and attention to detail as he did saltwater fishing.

Kadota took his 19-pound largemouth on January 8, 1989, six days after sending in his $40 entry fee for the *Bassin'* largemouth contest. A week after he had entered his big fish, he got his application and check back "with apologies." The envelope was shredded by a Post Office mail sorting machine. After considerable arguments, and some lawyers, the magazine's staff wouldn't allow Kadota's 19-pound fish to be entered. The entry fee had not, in fact, been delivered. This meant Kadota had lost out on the contest's $46,000 first prize. Lawyers geared up for action. Then, in December, Kadota caught his 15¾-pound bass and won. Litigation wasn't needed after all.

Kadota, who only fishes seriously in Castaic from December until April, says, "It's not a good idea to mess around with fish on nests. Besides, post-spawn fish don't break records."

Kadota, who knows Castaic as well as anyone, said, "Castaic should kick out the next world record. Eight or nine fish over 18 pounds were taken in the last few years. It's tough to fish though. It's at 2,500 acres at full pool, but it can be at 2,000 acres and dropping. It's also tough because there is so much fluctuation on water levels that you need to stay on the lake two to five days a week to remain effective. So you must know the lake well. Regulars and pros use aerial photos and very good depthfinders. Structure is very subtle and bass hold on quite small drop-offs so it's very demanding fishing."

All this action at Lake Castaic has adversely affected the previous No. 2 fish, a 21-pound, 3⅓-ounce hawg taken in 1980 by Raymond Easley from Lake Casitas, another southern California lake along the Pacific coast some 60 miles west of Lake Castaic. Easley still holds the IGFA and NFWFHF 8-pound line class records with that catch. His records appear fairly safe as Crupi, Arujo and Kadota all prefer working with heavier line.

3

Smallmouth Bass—Just Another Outing

Kentucky and Tennessee still argue about which state holds the world record for smallmouth bass. Both agree that David Hayes trolled his 11-pound, 15-ounce fish on a 600 series pearl-colored Bomber on July 9, 1955. Hayes said, "I caught it so close to the state line that I decided to let everyone have it." Hayes' casual attitude toward the location of his record extends to the location of the record-setting plug that he couldn't locate during a recent interview with an outdoor writer. Maybe 35 years is a long time to stay excited about a fish. Maybe he wasn't interested in the plug, a pearl Bomber with a set of hooks missing. Or, maybe he is just more interested in his other hobbies such as flying ultra-light aircraft.

Hayes' record, like many others, seemed almost accidental. Hayes, who turned 65 in 1990 and is now retired, took a day off from the family grocery business to take his wife and son fishing. Hayes said, "Dale Hollow Lake was down 15 or 20 feet during the five years or so before my record. This seemed to improve the fishing."

Hayes fished out of a 21-foot Lonestar aluminum cruiser with a 40-horsepower outboard. Hayes said he has since sold the boat because he spent too much time housekeeping it. It was extremely hot, well over 100 degrees by afternoon, so they made the 100-mile drive to the lake very early in the morning.

Then Hayes, his wife, Ruth, and his son, Don, backed their

cruiser out of its slip, and headed out on the lake toward a branch of the Wolf River near the Tennessee-Kentucky border. While Hayes liked to jig the banks, he elected to deep troll that lazy summer day with the family aboard. Hayes had three points picked out where he had caught a mix of spotted bass, walleyes and largemouth bass on past trips.

Hayes didn't really expect to troll up a smallmouth. Most of the fish he caught on regular weekend trips with his buddies, Morris Willis and W.B. Lowery, were walleyes, largemouth and spotted bass. Hayes said, "Smallmouth were rare."

As the boat left Cedar Hill Dock, Hayes dropped back his favorite Bomber on about 100 yards of line. Hayes said, "That made the plug run 15 to 16 feet deep on the 15- to 20-pound-test line I liked at the time." Hayes used a Penn 209 reel and one of the extremely durable, and rather clubby, short steel rods that trollers favored in the 1950s.

The day had started poorly. Hayes lost a large walleye with the net when Mrs. Hayes pulled the fish out of the water. So she retired from fishing for the day. Hayes decided to troll the rocky area where he had hooked the lost walleye.

Some Memories Never Fade

In 1973, *The Kentucky Angler* magazine, now defunct, asked Hayes to write about his 1955 record catch. Here's what Hayes remembered.

"We trolled along there two or three more times and then hit the place just right, I guess, and he hit it.

"I thought I was hung. I got down off the seat and loosened the drag on my reel in case I was hung. About that time he came up out of the water. He only jumped that one time, but he went about three feet.

"I began to take it easy with him. Evidently, when he came out and jumped, he tore one set of the treble hooks out of the plug, and the only thing holding him was one hook around one of his gills. It wasn't stuck in him, it was just in there holding him. I wore him down pretty good before I finally boated him. When I got him in the boat, I knew I had a big fish, but I didn't know he was that big ... "

Fisheries experts agree with a guide's statement that the Hayes smallmouth record would have topped 12 pounds had the fish been weighed immediately. Hayes only headed back to the dock in time to drive home in daylight. When he hit the dock at Cedar Hill and everyone realized the fish was a world record, a notary public certified the weight. Then, a Tennessee Fisheries biologist examined the fish—it turned out to be 13 years old. Since then the fish has been mounted, and then remounted in 1983. It's still on Hayes' wall, and the elusive plug lurks in his shop. But, as Hayes rather plaintively pointed out in a recent interview, "A lot of people, after I caught that fish, thought I ought to go out and catch a fish like that every time."

Today, while Hayes has two ponds on his 64 acres "for the local kids," he seldom fishes. "I sort of drifted away from fishing myself, but I'm hoping to get back to it this spring," he said. One wonders if that pearl 600 series Bomber will find its way back onto his line!

Perspectives

Hayes' fish, just an ounce shy of 12 pounds, looks even more impressive when you examine IGFA and NFWFHF line test records. Except for Paul E. Beal's 10½-pound fish taken with 8-pound test line from Dale Hollow in 1986, the range runs between 4 pounds, 12 ounces and 8 pounds, 6 ounces. Given this, Hayes's super smallmouth is almost twice as heavy as the average of other "record fish."

However, Billy Westmoreland, experienced smallmouth fisherman and well-known tackle company expert, took a 10½-pound smallmouth out of Dale Hollow Lake, and a 9½-pound "backup." The larger fish seems an especially fine trophy as it was caught on 4-pound-test line. In an *Outdoor Life* interview in 1980, Westmoreland mentioned a fish that " ... cast a spell over him and nearly drove him crazy for about eight months."

Westmoreland said, "There's no doubt about it. That brown fish had to weigh between 12 and 14 pounds. I had it up close enough to know that I had a world record. But I couldn't put it in the boat."

Fred McClintock, one of the top guides today on Dale Hollow Lake in Kentucky, said, "Things have changed since Hayes caught his record. Very few fishermen troll for smallmouth. We use grubs or Gitzits deep. Most of the big smallmouth we get run 6 or 7 pounds. Every so often someone gets an 8-pound or slightly larger fish. Hayes' fish must have gone over 12 pounds when he took it. We are lucky to see one fish over 9 pounds every few years."

However, Dale Hollow continues to produce NFWFHF and IGFA line class records. A. Paul Archer caught an 8-pound, 5-ounce fish on 6-pound test in 1987. Paul E. Beal took a 10-pound, 8-ounce fish in 1986 for the NFWFHF 8-pound line class record. Westmoreland gives part of the credit for the monstrous Dale Hollow fish to, " ... the abundance of crayfish. Crayfish make their homes along the shell banks and muddy points of Dale Hollow. You'll find the smallmouth where the crayfish are."

During the same 1980 interview, Westmoreland fitted in what may be the missing link to the massive smallmouth of that time. He said, "Of course, the U.S. Fish and Wildlife Service's decision several years ago to put 2 million rainbow trout fingerlings in the lake helped the smallmouth population, too. We all caught some of the biggest smallmouth we had taken in years. The smallmouth would come up, jump and belch out four or five rainbow fingerlings before the fishermen could get them in the boat. Then, after the smallmouths were put in the livewell we found several more fingerlings the fish had regurgitated."

Westmoreland continued, "That rainbow trout program was one of the biggest boons to big smallmouth fishing in recent times. But we could never talk the feds into putting the rainbows in again—even though we explained how much they helped the smallmouth fishing."

So, while Dale Hollow may be past its peak, Pickwick Lake in Alabama produced four NFWFHF line class records between 1987 and 1989. Pickwick Lake also holds the IGFA 4-pound line class record; a tie between a fish taken by Jim Rivers in 1987 and Sandy Jolley's 1989 fish, and the 16-pound line class record set by Terrell D. Nail in 1988.

4

Landlocked Striped Bass

When a local newspaper reporter called Ted Furnish for an interview the day after Furnish caught his 66-pound world record landlocked striper, Mrs. Furnish answered the phone. Mr. Furnish had gone fishing back at the O'Neill Forebay. Mrs. Furnish said, "Ted can sit there for eight hours and not catch anything and be totally happy. He goes out there to relax." In fact, Furnish was all set to cut his record fish up into steaks for dinner when Mrs. Furnish and their son talked him into mounting the fish.

Now the fish hangs at Grassland Sports in Los Banos, although it weighed in at 66 pounds two days after it was caught, the California Fish and Game experts who certified the fish as a state record, said, "Its minimum weight loss would have been at least 10 pounds." That, along with the dehydration you get when its 106 degrees out, might have pushed Albert McReynolds' striped bass all-tackle record of 78 pounds, 8 ounces.

During a recent interview, Furnish, a retired Army man, didn't seem particularly impressed with his record. He spent more time talking about the weather, O'Neill fishing, and other fish like the three, world-record fly rod tippet class stripers taken by his friend Al Whitehurst.

However, it soon became obvious that Furnish had carefully matched his gear selection and technique to his favorite fishing hole. This included the purchase of a huge net—a local bait shop employee who knows Furnish described it as being "mermaid-size."

Furnish rigged to troll with a Garcia 5½-foot bait rod, Garcia Ambassador 5000 reel and 14-pound-test Trilene line. This is about the standard trolling outfit in California for impoundment and delta stripers. Furnish trolls out of the Sea Swirl I/O with a 470 Mercruiser and uses a Humminbird fishfinder.

At the time, Trilene had an award program for records so Furnish's fish brought him in $10,000 for his world all-tackle record. Furnish didn't bother to mention this; he did note the "nice, gold-plated reel" Garcia sent after John Skrabo, then the Northern California Editor of *Fishing & Hunting News*, put Furnish in touch with the right people. Furnish also didn't mention that he holds the IGFA 16-pound line class, as well as the all-tackle world record.

Furnish did stress the importance of lure choice. When asked about the lure he carefully mentioned "a Cotton Cordell, broken back Jointed Spot that ran only ½ ounce. He even knew the model number—CJ27111—for his favorite silver with a black top finish.

"I only use the silver and black and yellow," Furnish said. "These match the size of the baitfish and run at just the right depth for my favorite areas. I drag them right over the rocks. I don't lose as many lures as most because the bill on the lure hits the rocks and flips the lure over. It's real important to get to the rocks. I think the big stripers must lie in the shade and wait for bait."

Mad Dogs And Fishermen

Furnish said that, besides being extremely hot, his record day didn't seem that different. His neighbor, Theo Alva, didn't get off from his street cleaning job until midmorning. So they got a noon start and met their buddies, Ernie and Joe, coming out with limits from the O'Neill Forebay below San Luis Reservoir, one of the holding waters for the California Aqueduct.

The 2,000-acre forebay offers more constant temperatures and better growth rates for stripers than the 13,800-surface-acre

Ted Furnish (right) got some help from a fishing buddy in showing off his 66-pound NFWFHF and IGFA all-tackle landlocked striped bass which was taken from the O'Neill Forebay, San Luis Reservoir near Los Banos, California.

San Luis Reservoir just to the west. Baitfish pumped down the California Aqueduct offer lots of food, and the area, while hot, dry and dusty all summer, is popular with campers in the colder months.

Furnish and Alva quickly launched their boat. "When you fish together several times a year, mechanics smooth out," Furnish said. "We headed to my favorite area right away. It's rocky and about 5 to 6 feet deep in spots, and drops to 10 feet in others." It was 2 o'clock, and 106 degrees—enough to drive less dedicated fishermen off the water—when the big fish hit.

"It didn't seem that big a fish to start," Furnish said. "It just never stopped. It kept circling and circling. I didn't touch the drag and we followed the fish around four circles a quarter or a half mile in diameter. One time I had nearly my whole line out.

Landlocked Striped Bass

I could see bare spool, but we were able to catch up. I still can't believe we took that fish on 15-pound test.

Furnish credits Alva's excellent boat handling with his landing the fish. "I yelled 'chase that fish,' but used some Army words," Furnish chortled, "I guess they worked.

"When it started to come up, the first thing I saw was the tail. It just waved back and forth. It was beautiful. I thought it was a mermaid—that's how big it was."

Alva managed to net the fish on the first pass. "We just sat there for about 10 minutes," Furnish said. "I was out of breath. After that we started screaming at each other. Then we'd do a high-five. Then look at the fish. It was so big it overlapped my net. Then we'd do more high-fives."

The huge striped bass stretched 2 inches over 4 feet long and 3 under a yard around. It clearly broke the old California record for striped bass set taken in 1951 from the San Joaquin River by Wendel Olson of Turlock.

Only after Furnish and Alva boated the fish, did things fall apart a bit. The fish lost lots of weight. It bled from 3:15 p.m. when it was landed until 10 a.m. the next day. "I put it on ice to stop the bleeding," Furnish says, "but Fish and Games says it still lost 10 pounds. I weighed the fish at home and it went 74 to 76 pounds, but we couldn't find a certified scale. We called everyone, but the television and radio people only got back in touch the next day when we finally got a certified scale."

More Records

More records should come out of O'Neill. Furnish hasn't given up on breaking his record even though drought conditions in California haven't improved the fishing in the last five years.

When interviewed recently he said, "Things had changed a bit, with low water most fellows are floating mud suckers on 20-pound test. I'm still trolling my Cordell Spots. Last month I took a 31-pound fish, and we get lots of 15- to 20-pound stripers. Every now and then we see a big return on the depthfinder. Some of the fellows think there are sturgeon. I'm hoping for a 70-pound striper. I know where to find a certified scale right away now."

Art Whitehurst would agree with his friend, Ted Furnish.

Al Whitehurst set an IGFA fly rod 16-pound tippet class record with this 54-pound, 8-ounce landlocked striped bass, taken from the O'Neill Forebay.

Whitehurst holds the 16-pound test tippet NFWFHF and IGFA fly rod record for striped bass with a 54-pound, 8-ounce fish taken on September 17, 1989, from the forebay. Whitehurst says, "Records for 2-, 4-, 6-, 8-, 10- and 12-pound tippets are all under 20 pounds and well within range."

Furnish may get another chance to break the record, too. Few fishermen could offer such a combination of skill, intensive knowledge of a limited area, time to fish and, most of all, angler optimism that defines a positive mental attitude!

Handling Hybrid Hassles

In many Southern reservoirs with white bass populations, hybrid bass, a cross between striped and white bass, remain a good possibility in many Southeastern states. Reports of "decent" stripers filleted for dinner that turned out to be record-class hybrids seem to be everywhere.

Any medium to large striper with the suspicion of broken lateral lines (the dark stripes) should be carefully checked by a fisheries biologist. If the fish turns out to be a hybrid, it could set a world record for all-tackle or line class.

Hybrid records show rapid growth. The current IGFA record, a 24-pound, 3-ounce hybrid taken May 12, 1989, at

Landlocked Striped Bass   43

Leesville Lake by David Lambert, shows the typical broken stripe key to identification. At least one larger fish, misidentified as a striper, has been eaten by a fisherman who missed a chance at a world record.

History

It's interesting, indeed, how Furnish's fish arrived at the O'Neill Forebay. To start, one of its ancestors rolled west across the United states in the water car on a transcontinental train in the 1870s when the first two small stockings of stripers were released into the California delta to spread as far north as Washington and south to Southern California. After many, many generations, Furnish's fish probably slipped through the screens of the canal that sends water from the northern California delta to southern California. Such water is stored in the O'Neill Forebay. Some, when not needed by the "thirsty south", is pumped up into a larger reservoir to be released as needed. With the current drought, "pumping up" isn't possible, so there are grave concerns about striper survival in the delta and in reservoirs that are warmed by low water conditions to the point where stripers that need lots of oxygen to flourish, may be in trouble.

Reservoirs, it should be noted, got landlocked stripers started back before World War II when the Navy, anxious for power, dammed the Santee and Cooper Rivers in South Carolina in such haste that trapped stripers remained, and remain to this day in Lakes Marian and Moultrie. At present, the best striper fishing in the world is inland, in deeper, colder reservoirs like those in Tennessee where millions of small stripers are stocked each year.

The 100-Pound Striper

Stripers over 100 pounds have been taken with nets in saltwater. Records list a 112-pound striper caught at Orleans, Massachusetts, and a famous set of fish that all weighed about 125 pounds that were caught at Edentown, North Carolina. All of these were, of course, females. Ideal striper growth requires several things. First, water about 64 degrees—some studies suggest that bigger fish need progressively colder water. Even more important, stripers require at least three parts per million

This 60-pound striped bass was taken by Robert Byer on a topwater Cordell Pencil Popper from the Yuba River in California.

Landlocked Striped Bass

dissolved oxygen. Given these conditions, and the absence of predation from seals, sharks and such in freshwater, landlocked stripers would theoretically grow to larger sizes than saltwater fish. Such has not so far proved to be the case with records, but the spread narrows.

Perspective

With a 60-pound, 8-ounce IGFA line class record landlocked striper from Melton Hill Lake, Tennessee, caught in 1988 by Gary Helms, and a 60-pound fish caught by Robert R. Byer on a Cordell pencil Popper with 12-pound-test line from the Feather River in California, it's quite clear that Furnish's record may not stand for long. Such is particularly the case in light of the five saltwater record stripers over 70 pounds and well-documented reports of netted stripers of 85, 93 and over 100 pounds.

At least two reports from knowledgable observers on Tennessee reservoirs that get massive striper stockings and offer ideal growth patterns suggest that 80-, 90- or even 100-pound stripers are possible in freshwater. However, these massive fish may feed on pound or 2-pound baitfish. So they might not be interested in typical plug sizes. One expert suggests "big suckers and other huge minnows that might weigh 2 or 3 pounds like the trophy northern pike pros freelined down to the 64-degree or slightly cooler depths that a few, doubtless scattered *super stripers* patrol."

Some suggest that a good way to do this would be still fishing or slowly wind-drifting over rocky bottom with a temperature-controlled downrigger with a line release setup to a huge bait like the 2-foot-long suckers muskie fishermen use.

5

Puzzling Walleye Trophy

alleye addicts from the upper Midwest would find Mabry Harper's attitude puzzling. In fact, that's just one of many unusual features about this record. Mabry Harper, from Hartsville, Tennessee, caught a 25-pound walleye from Old Hickory Lake near Nashville on August 1, 1960. Fortunately, a rather grainy snapshot of Harper's wife holding the fish exists. According to the record books, the fish was 41 inches long with a 29-inch girth. Harper took the fish on 75-pound-test line, and it supposedly took about 50 minutes to land.

Harper must have had the world's loosest line drag. Walleye, particularly big walleye, don't pull that hard. Harper, in his 60s when he caught his record fish, isn't available. He died in 1970. Contemporary newspaper accounts noted that he was a plumber, fishing on his day off, and he took the fish home and ate it. So fishermen who want to see the catch may have to attend one of tournament pro Mike McClelland's walleye seminars or fishing shows where a replica of the record fish is exhibited.

It's not unusual that rumors abound. Tom Rollins, an official at Old Hickory Reservoir, says, "My recollection is rather dim, and much information second- and third-hand. I heard that the big walleye, a female, was a brood-sow breeder released from the hatchery just below Dale Hallow Dam. Nobody really pays much attention to walleyes here."

Barbara Purvis of the Fish Management Division said, "We didn't get decent records until 1977. All paperwork on the old records are gone." Confusion about the catch starts with the Tennessee records. They list August 3, 1960, as the record date. Did Harper wait 48 hours before weighing his fish? This seems unlikely, but it does raise some questions. Two questions are central, why was the fish so huge and why haven't fish in the same size range come out of Old Hickory since?

Dave Woodard, chief information specialist for Tennessee Fish and Game, said, "Harper's record will never be equaled in Tennessee. His fish was one of the old river-strain walleyes. When reservoirs like Old Hickory filled, all the new food pumped up the river fish sizes. Prior to that you were lucky to catch a 9- or 10-pound walleye. The fishery flourished for a few years; then started trailing off as the reservoir matured. The river-strain fish don't seem to have survived.

"Kentucky had the same problem. They tried for 20 years to recreate the river fishery in Lake Cumberland. Never did. We are now getting walleye populations back, but different strains dominate."

What Walleye?

It's also bothersome that Harper's catch got so little attention in Tennessee. Clearly, fishermen in Tennessee, Arkansas and other more southern states with river and impoundment walleyes have a rather different attitude toward these fish than walleye addicts in the Upper Midwest. Southerners simply do not take walleye fishing seriously. As will be seen, this opens up a window of record opportunity for traveling walleye pros from "walleye" states!

Today's Record Water

A quick check of IGFA records shows the 8-, 12- and 16-pound line test records were set at Greers Ferry Lake, Arkansas, and the 4-pound and 20-pound line test records were set on the North Little Red River and the Devils Fork in Heber Springs. A call to Arkansas Fish and Game officials turned up the fact that all of these records came out of Greers Ferry Lake or its tributaries. Close examination of the records showed three fish were taken in March—two on the same day, the 14th!

Mary Harper, wife of the late Mabry Harper, held her husband's record catch in this photo taken in 1960 just after her husband had pulled this 25-pound lunker out of Old Hickory Lake in Tennessee.

—one in January and one in February. This suggests a schedule for record seekers!

Phone interviews turned up another coincidence. Al Nelson, who caught the 12-pound IGFA line class record with a 22-pound, 11-ounce fish, and Erma Windorff, who captured the 8-pound IGFA record with a 19-pound, 5-ounce fish, were friends and, more important, had both fished extensively for walleye in the Upper Midwest.

An Arkansas fish and game spokesman said, "Greers Ferry now holds the world record walleye. It will probably die of old age. If you look at the records, you'll see they were all taken just before spawning. Most of these are up at the river mouths during the Fairfield Bay fishing contest. That's got a $20 entrance fee, big money prizes and, lately, for a world record walleye, a $1,000,000 bonus.

"If you look at the records, you'd think that's the time to fish. Maybe so, but that's the only time fishermen really hit walleyes. Nobody really fishes correctly for them the rest of the year. So most are caught milling around off river mouths or on spawning runs. Greers Ferry is a tough lake, so you need to be very smart, or very lucky to score on walleyes consistently.

"One of the big problems for locals who are not experienced

Puzzling Walleye Trophy   49 walleye fishermen is the very low concentration of walleyes that's balanced by their very large sizes. This is because the species is relatively unfished except on spawning runs."

Greers Ferry Fundamentals

Greers Ferry Lake is really the star of today's line test and tomorrow's potential all-tackle record walleye picture. It started to fill in 1962. So today, it is a fairly sterile lake because of age and topography. It's rather unusual for southern lakes, as it averages over 100 feet deep between the rolling hills of the Ozark Plateau. It's formed by two large basins connected by "the narrows," a prime spot for walleye where the lake is only 400 to 500 yards wide.

Other species—striped, white, hybrid, Kentucky, small-mouth and largemouth bass—are present, but not in very high densities. One expert said, "On most waters 10 percent of the area has 90 percent of the fish. At Greers Ferry, it's one percent!"

Even so, the IGFA line test records for Greers Ferry were mostly set in 1982 and 1983. Because the reservoir filled in 1962, these fish might be at the end of the lifespan of fish hatched at that time. Encouragingly though, there is one 1989 record over 20 pounds.

Nelson's New Record

Al Nelson's record is still the Arkansas State, IGFA 12-pound and NFWFHF 10-pound line test record. Nelson, an experienced walleye fisherman from Illinois, had heard about his friend Erma Windorff's 19-pound, 5-ounce monster. He had paid his $20 entry fee in the annual contest put on by Fairfield Communities, so he planned to fish "day and night" if he had to. Nelson was a deputy sheriff. So his shifts permitted odd hours. That's how he found himself out alone on the lake in a duck boat that spring. He had two lines out (legal in Arkansas) tolling with Bombers, but he kept hanging up. He turned out to deeper water, but hung up again.

As Nelson told it to an outdoor magazine interviewer, "I didn't bother to grab that rod because I figured it was hung up on a log. I brought in the other line first, then aimed my boat at the one still fouled. When it pulled back, I knew I had a fish

While this 12-pound, 8-ounce walleye would only qualify for an IGFA line class record if it had been taken on 2-pound-test line, it holds the distinction of having been caught on a plug specifically designed for muskie fishing!

on, but figured it was a small one that had probably tangled up with a snag."

Some snag! After 20 minutes and a couple of strong runs, the walleye came up alongside the boat, spent, on its side, and ready to net. Unfortunately, he didn't have time to grab a net.

"Because my duck boat is so low to the water," Nelson said, "I just reached out with my right hand and grabbed the fish under the gill, then dropped the rod and hauled it (the fish) into the boat with both hands. That's when my heart really started pounding. I figured that I'd better get the fish to shore before I tipped the boat over in my excitement."

When Nelson finally reached the Fairfield Bay Marina after a drive through thick fog, he expected the fish to weigh close to 20 pounds. Nelson said, "When we put it onto the scale, the needle just went up and up and up, taking my heart with it."

Nelson's catch was the second largest walleye ever caught. It weighed 22 pounds, 11 ounces and measured 3 feet long with a 22-inch girth. It's now mounted in the Fairfield Bay Marina to inspire other contest participants, for Nelson's $20 investment returned over $11,000 in prizes.

Windorff's Lawn Chair Special

Nelson's entry beat out Erma Windorff's walleye, the fish that inspired Nelson's efforts, for the yearly prizes. Windorff's fish was a "lawn chair special." The Windorffs had set up their lawn chairs, slipped on their snowmobile suits and settled down to wait for fish on the night of March 2, 1982. They still fished their shiner minnow baits with 6-pound test on identical "K-Mart" rods. Suddenly—she still doesn't know why—Erma asked her husband to change seats, and outfits. Her next cast produced what was then the third largest walleye ever caught.

The fish rolled early in the fight. So Erma played it carefully for 20 minutes. Elmer did his bit and waded into the frigid water as far as possible to net the fish. The Windorffs, with the contest in mind, dropped the whopper walleye into a big sack and shot off for the weighing station. The fish, still alive when weighed, was the same length as Nelson's catch, but a bit smaller in girth so it weighed *only* 19 pounds, 5 ounces.

Perspectives

After record catches slackened following Mark Wallace's 18-pound, 4-ounce 1984 catch, experts—mostly from other waters—suggested that Greers Ferry had peaked. Tom Evans' 20-pound, 9-ounce fish caught in 1989 suggests they may be wrong. The problem seems more a lack of skilled walleye efforts than a lack of record-size walleye. Walleye specialists might take note.

6

The Muskie Wars

When Jim Corbett, the legendary hunter of man-eating big cats, was asked to describe the most important thing about hunting, he replied, "It is that there should be a clear understanding about who is stalking who." This isn't always the case with muskies. Any fish big enough to eat a beaver, even a small one, demands respect. Still, like pike, before World War II muskies were considered unwelcome predators by walleye and trout fishermen. Dumping a green muskie with teeth sharp enough to strip paint off plugs into a boat didn't seem sensible either. So many early catches were disqualified when they were shot before being taken from the water.

By World War II, the sheer size of big muskies made them a prized catch, and the piscatorial record wars raged between New York and Wisconsin as the all-tackle record changed hands. New York won this war due, in large part, to the efforts of Leonard and the late Betty Hartman, and of Art and Ruth Lawton, two married couples who traded muskie records.

Art Lawton still holds the all-tackle muskellunge record with a 69-pound, 15-ounce fish. His wife, Ruth, retains the unlimited line class record at 68 pounds, 5 ounces. Leonard Hartman, their contemporary and neighbor, and Betty Hartman caught over 3,600 muskies, but lost the Leonard and Hartman muskie wars that raged through the pages of *Field & Stream* yearly fishing contests from World War II well into the

1960s. Hartman, who once held the world record, now only has the 4-, 6-, 8- and 10-pound line class NFWFHF power trolling records. All of Betty Hartman's records have been broken, including her largest: a 64-pound, 4-ounce fish she caught alone without a net or a gaff. In 1986, she was elected to the National Fresh Water Fishing Hall of Fame. She died in 1990.

Of course, if Wisconsin's Malo Muskie, caught in 1954, had not been shot, and had been properly weighed, it might have the record. At that, it's the largest mounted muskie and listed by the NFWFHF as the "unofficial" 70-pound record. Art Lawton didn't mount his record fish. He gave it to his brother to eat!

Still, if Lawton hadn't, for some unexplained reason, waited 30 hours before he weighed his fish, his would have gone well over 70 pounds. You could make a case that really big muskies turn the minds of otherwise rational fishermen to mush. Those too restless to wait (Canadian biologists say the average "experienced" muskie fisherman waits 100 hours per legal fish) often suggest that the boredom between hits causes the problem. Less charitable types note that rational fishermen have little interest in catching fish that eat things as odd as ducks, blackbirds and small beavers.

Even allowing this, can you imagine eating a fish you knew was a world record? Especially since taxidermists only charged about a dollar an inch for mounting in those days.

As Lawton explained in a later interview, "I don't care for mounted fish. I had two of my early muskies put up, and they're gathering dust in the attic now. Ruth and I don't fish for mounted trophies; we're after the fun and thrills of battling the biggest freshwater gamefish in North America."

Lawton's battles extended to more than muskies. A neighbor of the Lawtons and Hartmans, Al Russel, said Art Lawton, who habitually trolled the Boundary Waters of the St. Lawrence River with his wife, Ruth, had a long standing contest with Leonard Hartman and his wife, Betty. The Lawtons usually won the *Field & Stream* contest that then handled record keeping, and the couples competed for ink by taking out rival outdoor writers. So their angling exploits were well-advertised nationally.

Russel also said, "Both couples were subject to many local

Tom Rosenberger holds the mounted 30-pound muskie which he caught in 1989. The 47½-inch fish is an Indiana state record. Rosenberger caught it on a Rebel Jointed Minnow.

rumors." Now, nearly 50 years later, it's difficult to figure out exactly what happened. Apparently, Len Hartman had the record at 68 pounds. The week Art Lawson set the record, he had hooked and released several muskies. Lawson reported, "We released muskies without touching them by slipping the gaff between the plug and the hooks and flipping the hooks free." Recent tests suggest this is more difficult than one might expect from the simple description. This is especially the case if you look at the massive Slim Wizz and other huge plugs hung with stout treble hooks favored at the time. Still, if anyone could do it, Lawton could. His string of records is astonishing.

Lawton caught his first muskie, a 25-pounder, in 1936. He started fishing with Ruth before they were married in 1939. They fished together well past 1959.

Lawton's big fish string started in 1944 when he won the national contest for the top muskie with a 53-pounder. In 1948, he won with a 58-pound, 5-ounce fish. He knew there were bigger muskies.

In 1955, he took top spot in the country with a 58-pound muskie. In 1956, his wife won the contest with a 60-pound muskie caught Labor Day weekend. Leonard was runner-up with a 52-pound muskie. Lawton's 1957 fish remains the record, but, given the evidence, he might have known the location of an even larger fish that he expected to troll up.

The Master Troller

While today's muskie experts usually cast plugs, Lawton had perfected power trolling, the system that so suited the rather heavier, and definitely more difficult to cast, muskie gear of his time. Lawton and his wife, Ruth, preferred to eat walleyes. So they didn't keep many muskies, but they were definitely self-admitted "lunker addicts" who spent over 20 years specializing in trolling for muskies. The Lawtons worked out their unique systems over these years.

In an article he wrote for *Outdoor Life* in 1959, Lawton noted, "Big muskies lie deep, which is one reason we do all our fishing by trolling. You can cast for them, but we've never caught a good one that way. It's hard to get a casting lure down to where you have to go."

He continued, "You're not going to take muskies unless you fish deliberately for them. As a starter, that means tackle heavy enough for the job at hand ... "

Lawton and his wife, Ruth, used 5½- to 6-foot-long medium-stiff steel or glass rods. They didn't favor any particular reel as long as it had a reliable drag and was big enough to hold at least 150 yards of 20-pound-test nylon line. They usually trolled with 125 feet of line out and 100 yards on the spool, and "more than once needed all the reserve." Terminal tackle included plugs from 6 inches to 12 inches long, snapped to a 30- to 36-inch-long braided steel leader. Such rigs, absent the clunky steel rods, would work nicely today.

Monster Muskie

The Lawtons' record 1957 fall week was outstanding even

for such experts. As it drew to a close on September 21, Lawton and his wife took 20- and 28-pound fish. They had, with their usual trolling system, hooked 30 muskies and lost five. Thirty muskies are more muskies than most fishermen will ever land in a lifetime!

The next day, Sunday, September 22, 1957, turned out to be perfect. Lawton said, "Such days were overcast and cool with a slight riffle on the water." This allows trollers to spot ledges and weedbeds, but obscures the vision of the muskie enough so it sees the plug, not the boat.

After about four hours of trolling, Lawton's rod snapped down just as they passed a grassy island. He claimed that "Ruth and I could tell in an instant a muskie takes whether it's in the 20-pound class or over 40 pounds. This one was a lunker. The strike felt like snagging bottom."

Lawton's fish fought deep for nearly half an hour. Lawton, with Ruth's help, kept the fish in the deeper channels and could barely follow it to free his line from weeds and snags. Even so, for the first 30 minutes the muskie was in charge.

When the fish came to the top, it tried to jump. Lawton said, " ... he couldn't get his big belly out of the water. After that he stayed near the top." Lawton kept the pressure on, and his experience finally told. After a fight that lasted just over an hour, he finally hauled the fish into the boat.

Unlike many muskie fishermen at the time, Lawton neither shot nor clubbed his muskies before he boated those he intended to keep. His system could work today. He would play the fish close, and then rap the boat. If the fish had any fight left, he'd dart away. Lawton did use a very heavy gaff. He rather caustically commented, "If you're hunting for bear, go loaded for bear ... If you're fishing for muskie, carry a heavy gaff."

Lawton knew the fish that lay in the bottom of his boat was the biggest muskie he had caught, and he had probably caught more muskies over 50 pounds than any man living. So it's bothersome that he did not immediately weigh the fish. Lawton said, "It didn't occur to us that he might be a world record. If it had, we wouldn't have delayed the weighing as long as we did. We always waited until we got home to weigh fish. So that's what we did. We packed the fish in the truck and drove 200 miles home."

Nearly 30 hours later, Lawton finally weighed his fish at a slaughterhouse. Then, he hung the fish in his yard for the neighbors to admire before he gave it to his brother, Ernest, to eat. The fish drew 100 or so spectators. So why didn't Lawton mount the fish? In a later interview, he said, "When I saw that he was only one ounce shy of 70 pounds, my eyes almost popped out of my head. At last, I had the granddad I'd been hoping to catch for 20 years." Fisheries experts suggest 30 hours of shrinkage could have been more than five pounds and possibly more. One must wonder why Lawton did not weigh his fish immediately.

His neighbor Al Russel's scale only ran up to 25 pounds— Russel has some interesting tales to tell about some fish weighed by others on that scale. Still, there were certified scales at the Clayton store near the Lawton cabin. Considering the number of prize-winning muskies Lawton had caught over the years, he had to know that this fish was outstanding. Now, it exists only in replica.

Could it be that Lawton, as Al Russel said in a recent interview, had an even larger muskie located? Muskies do tend to stay in the same area. If this was the case, then Lawton was confident that he could catch such a fish. Did he figure it was a waste of money to mount a record he planned to break soon?

Lawton did claim that he and his wife had no "secret fishing hole" where they caught most of their fish. He claimed to fish the American side of the St. Lawrence from seven miles above Clayton to eight miles below town. He cited "a dozen places" where they took fish.

7

Europe's Lock On Record Pike

Pike get and give no quarter. Except for the lowly burbot, the pike is the only freshwater fish native to both hemispheres. So it is strong testimony to their survival skills that they flourish even where past methods include shooting, choking, netting, stranding, gaffing, nightlining, marooning, stunning, pitchforking and trimming —the last being a sort of Britannic jug fishing.

The "sporting" British did worse than that, too! In 1801, the Reverend W. B. Daniel, in his book *Rural Sports*, suggested that readers tie a minnow-baited line to a goose foot and let the goose haul the pike into the bank! The Reverend Daniel noted, "The goose usually won." With such arcane methods, it's no wonder that of the top 100 pike of all time, Europeans have captured 99!

Still, Americans can't tout their sportsmanship, either. Vermont has a short season where pike are shot off beds during spawning!

North American Records

The only American pike to break into the top 100 is Peter Dubuc's 46-pound, 2-ounce fish, the current North American record. It was caught more than 50 years ago, in 1940, from New York's Great Sacandaga Lake. Ron Kolodziej, a well-known outdoor writer and guide on the lake, said, "No photo of the fish exists. I've looked for photos for a couple of years. I heard Dubuc didn't want to pay $52.50 to have his fish stuffed and mounted. So he ate the fish. He died, and I can't even find the relatives."

While details seem lost in the confusion of World War II, and a few skeptics doubt the size of the fish, it seems well-authenticated. Since it cost $1 an inch to mount fish then, the fish was 52½ inches long.

"Dubuc owned a cabin on the lake and was a regular on the water," Kolodziej said. "A compulsive fisherman, he also tied for the New York state largemouth record. He reportedly took the fish on 12-pound-test line with a 4-foot, copper-wire leader. Nobody knows the exact details except that the fight lasted nearly an hour."

Since the fish was almost certainly a female—big pike almost without exception are females—it could have contained 2 or 3 pounds of eggs just before spawning. Nobody bothered to check out the cleaned weight. So the fish could have been holding 3 to 6 pounds of ingested baitfish, too. The weight seems to be consistent with the length.

A recent 39-pound catch from the lake, by Gino Terenzetti, supports the measurements and weight of the Dubuc pike. The fish, taken in May, had just spawned and, except for Terenzetti's 10-inch-long sucker, was empty. Add in 2 or 3 pounds of eggs and a baitfish one-third the pike's 51-inch length that might weigh 3 or 4 pounds. If it were a walleye, that size might have added 6 pounds. Pike, it should be noted, prefer prey species about one-third their length. Given these considerations Dubuc's record seems more than possible.

Other big Great Sacandaga pike seem possible, too. In a 1984 State of New York Department of Environmental Conservation publication, Phil Johnson reported on Great Sacandaga's pike. He cited the claims of a Mr. Cornell, a local and trophy fisherman who had landed at least 20 pike 40 inches or longer.

"I was fishing late on a windy, rainy day in early May," Cornell said. "I had caught and released one fish that measured 38 inches. When rerigging the line, I decided to try as bait a 24-inch-long sucker I had been saving.

"When the pike hit, it nearly cleared all the line from my reel. Then it stopped. I thought I had lost the fish so I just reeled in steadily, figuring the resistance at the other end was just the bait being dragged through the water. But it wasn't.

"The reel was almost fully rewound when I saw the pike. It apparently saw the boat at the same instant. It rolled over and took off. I honestly believe it was 60 inches long. No freshwater fish in the world could break that line on a straight run. That pike did."

Johnson said, "Using a generally accepted formula for estimating a pike—length in inches cubed, divided by 3,500—if the fish was 60 inches long, it would have weighed approximately 61 pounds." That may sound a bit optimistic until you learn that John Carrol's line was new 60-pound test!

So Great Sacandaga, a 29-mile-long reservoir with 125 miles of shoreline, may hold the largest North American pike. It's ideal habitat with flooded marshes, extensive shallows and a huge population of big suckers and other trash fish ideally sized for monster pike.

Echoing Carrol, Kolodziej said, "Great Sacandaga's shallow waters and many snags protect pike because few fishermen fish with the right baits at the right time. When I guide I use a lot of downrigger methods during the heat of summer. Those new to the area can find it tough fishing because levels vary so much. If you go with a guide, or know the lake, you can expect good northerns. In fact, 15-pound fish are nothing unusual."

The Terenzetti brothers, Gino and Americo, would testify to that. They spend two weeks watching two lines each after the first Saturday in May when the pike season opens on Great Sacandaga Lake. Fifteen times one or both Terenzetti's have ranked in the top five in the annual beer company New York State fishing contest. One year, Americo landed a 49-inch-long, 36-pound fish. He didn't win. Brother Gino beat him with a 39-pound, 4-ounce, 51-inch trophy. This was the biggest pike caught in Great Sacandaga since Dubuc's 1940 fish. Of the 11 New York pike that ran over 30 pounds in the contest's history, nine came from Great Sacandaga. That's definitely one spot to try if you want to break the North American record.

In the Western Hemisphere, the most productive areas for large pike are the southern portions of Saskatchewan, Manitoba and the northern portions of adjacent U.S. border states. One of these states, Vermont, offers the American version of an aquatic Vietnam fire fight for 10 days every spring. Vermont, an otherwise sensible state, allows fishermen to slog or canoe through the flooded shallows around Lake Champlain. Spawning pike are easily seen because their dorsal fins stick out of the water. The pike are shot with handguns or shotguns loaded with slugs! This is supposedly a test of marksmanship and good judgment because a pike's dorsal is near the tail, and you need to pop a round into the water near the head so the concussion stuns or kills the pike. Then, it's humanely dispatched and either pickled or smoked to dissolve the many small bones that otherwise threaten digestion.

European Pike

While European pike are definitely larger than American species, there has been much nonsense written about pike sizes on both sides of the Atlantic. We hear about an 80-pound, 4-foot pike from Sweden that "was dragged five times up to the gunwale of the punt, but never captured." Then, there is the famous Mannheim pike that hung in the Cathedral of the same name that was supposed to have lived for 267 years. Skeptic H.G. Seeley, writing about northern pike in 1886, noted, " ... preserved in the cathedral of Mannheim, its bones furnished the unexpected gloss on the old story that it had been manufactured out of smaller fishes." Another European source mentions a 350-pound pike that was 19 feet long. That must have looked like a broomstick. In proper pike proportions, it would have weighed over a ton!

Though pike eat anything, they don't get that big. Their diet includes oddments such as baby ducks, swimming mice and muskrats. Pike are considerable predators of baby waterfowl in the spring. They certainly define the word "predator." One guide said, "It's not unknown for pike to be boated that are not hooked, just locked in a death grip on lures or flies."

Even stranger tales exist abroad. In 1865, a 40-pound, 49-inch-long pike was hauled in when it hit the head of a floating croquet mallet that was tied to a string and tossed into an estate pond by the 3-year-old son of the Devon estate's owner. There is even an English story of a pike found dead in a haystack. His teeth were set into the hind leg of a dead fox. The story suggests the pike attacked the fox before it was dragged from the water. The English do like country tales!

The Irish have even more pike stories. That's fair; they have more pike. Many of these early big fish were caught in Ireland's Lough—lakes—or rivers. Few were caught on rods. It was only after the 14th century when German armorers developed the art of drawing wire that reliable wire leaders became available and bigger fish could be taken by more sporting methods. Horsehair leaders don't cut it with pike!

John Buller, in his British book, *Pike And The Pike Angler*, lists at least 34 Irish and English pike ranging in size from 92 pounds down to the weight of the current North American record fish. A recent magazine listing reported 99 fish larger than Dubuc's North American record. Some of these records —the list goes back to 1822—are a bit obscure. A number of these are well-documented. Pike approaching muskie-size may be the occasional result of the combination of ideal conditions and a lack of angling pressure.

The World Record Pike

Clearly, even bigger pike swim in Europe than in the British Isles. The NFWFHF current world record, a monster 55-pound, 15-ounce pike came from Czechoslovakia's Lipno Reservoir, where at least six other pike over 38 pounds were taken in the last 20 years.

Jiri Blaha took his 4½-foot-long pike on a large roach bait—a European minnow much like our sucker. According to the report in *Splash*, the magazine of the NFWFHF, the 55-pound, 15-ounce pike was landed without a net or gaff. All records were carefully checked. The scale examination, weigh-in and angler and witness interviews were done by Bedrich Hala, a Czech magazine editor. So this fish is now the NFWFHF all-tackle record.

The IGFA world record northern pike is Lothar Louis' 55-pound, 1-ounce fish from Grefeern Lake, Germany. Both European fish are larger than the North American record. Even larger fish await lucky fishermen in the USSR. A standard guide to Soviet freshwater fish lists netted pike from the Dniepr marshes at approximately 131 pounds, and a 69-pound fish from

Lake Il'men which is near Novgorod.

Even farther east, the Amur pike, now stocked in a few U.S. waters, runs slightly smaller, but, according to international experts, "it fights harder." Pennsylvania and one or two other states have experimented with this species.

Few of these pike species got much attention in the past. European trout and salmon fishing is almost entirely private and extremely expensive. Carp or perch are commercially raised in ponds or netted. So pike are considered useless predators. Water bailiffs try to destroy them by any means at hand and convert them, depending on the country, into fish cakes or garden fertilizer as soon as possible. So, well-documented pike records are only now starting to surface in Europe.

Perspectives

A trip to Ireland after some careful research on Irish Loughs could produce a record. For pike grow fast there, as well as elsewhere under ideal conditions. A 41-pound Irish pike had only eight annual rings on its gill covers!

A visit to Sweden could produce a record, too. Swedish catches hold the IGFA 4-, 12-, 16-, 20- and 30-pound line class records. Jan Eggers, one of the most expert pike fishermen in Europe, touts the Trosa Archipelago about 75 miles south of Stockholm, Sweden, as the best choice. Of course, he may be a bit prejudiced; when he first fished the area over 25 years ago, he caught 47 pike on his first day.

Trosa pike are extremely fat because they live on Baltic herring. Still, with a week's efforts, and a good guide, a 30-pound pike is a definite possibility and 20-pound pike are common in the shallows, sandbars, rocks and bays of the skerry coast. These pike are so big that a 6-inch-long Swim Wizz, usually used for muskie, and other monster plugs are popular lures. With the catch-and-release method common in Europe, some outstanding pike are certain. In America,

Great Sacandaga is the spot to try for a North American record.

8

Blue Catfish—Mistaken Identity

On Tuesday evening, September 23, 1959, the Yankton (S.D.) Press and Dakotan ran a rather grainy photo with the following caption:

"CLAIMS CATFISH RECORD. Ed Elliot of Vermillion, left, displays the 97-pound, record-breaking silver channel catfish which he caught in the Missouri River near Gayville last week. The whopper, which measured 57 inches in length and 37 inches around the middle, weighed 2½ pounds more than the largest catfish ever caught on a rod and reel. Pictured with Elliot is Charles Gray of Vermillion, who has caught more than 250 catfish weighing 65 pounds or more during his fishing days and who pioneered the idea of fishing big catfish with a rod and reel. It was he who led Elliot to the deep hole in the Missouri where the record-breaker was caught."

It took a long letter from James T. Shields, then South Dakota's Superintendent of Fisheries, to convince Elliot that his fish was, in fact, a blue catfish rather than a "silver channel," apparently a local nickname for these fish. Catfish and bullhead identification remains a problem. For example, the IGFA does not recognize the fish the NFWFHF lists as the black bullhead all-tackle world record. However, Shields made a good case for the angular fin and 30 to 35 rays of the blue catfish rather than the rounded anal fin and its 24 to 29 rays characteristic of the channel catfish. IGFA and NFWFHF agreed. Elliot was apparently harder to convince.

In a 1964 letter to the South Dakota Department of Game, Fish and Parks, Mike Bell, who then ran the *Field & Stream* fishing contest noted, " … the angler thought the fish was a silver channel catfish … Mr. Elliot accepted that decision, although I think he still was not completely convinced the fish was a blue catfish."

Eventually, Elliot changed his mind and, somewhat reluctantly, agreed his record was, in fact, a blue catfish. Elliot hasn't seen the need to change much else. When interviewed in 1991, he noted that he "had the same phone number, house and wife that he had when he caught his record fish and entered it in the 1959 *Field & Stream* contest." He won big!

Like many modest record holders, he cites the help of a mentor who, he said, "should have had the record. Charlie Gray caught more big catfish on a rod and reel than any man living or dead. I was lucky to fish with him. We fished together for years, and we always caught fish."

Elliot continued, "I'd heard of Charlie for years before I met him. You'd hear about Charlie all the time, and the stories were always about 75- to 100-pound catfish. He used to fish for the market with trot lines, but we switched to rod and reel after we started fishing together."

Elliot and Gray fished from a 10-by-26-foot "barrel barge," a home-made, platform-type boat well suited to stand-up fishing on the Missouri River. Elliot and Gray were lucky enough to fish in one of its few remaining natural bank sections of the no longer so "mighty" Missouri. The stretch alternates between deep holes and shallows, and divides South Dakota and Nebraska.

"We were," Elliot said, "pretty advanced for the time." They powered their homemade craft with an 18-horsepower Johnson motor. At the time, most catfishermen used sturdy handlines, jugs or trotlines; Elliot and Gray rigged up with heavy ocean rods, and Penn level-wind reels filled with 100 yards of 80-pound-test line. "More line was not needed," Elliot said, "because catfish tend to sulk deep when hooked, and only reluctantly move out of their favorite holes."

Huge 9/0 Eagle Claw hooks jammed through hunks of carp "as big as your fist" and rigged on 76-pound-test leaders were held on bottom by at least 2 ounces of lead. At times, more

Edward Elliot's 97-pound blue catfish holds the all-tackle record in both the IGFA and NFWFHF record books. This record fish was taken from the Missouri River in southeastern South Dakota.

Blue Catfish—Mistaken Identity

lead was needed because currents ran seven or eight miles an hour; other times they went up to pound sinkers.

However, by properly positioning their barrel barge at the head of holes and securing it with a big anchor, the two catfish specialists could let the boat's swing move their baits back and forth to cover the entire hole. Catfish would smell the bait and, like crayfish after a slice of bacon, would move upstream to take a bite.

Gray had discovered that the presence of smaller catfish from "arm- to leg-size" mean big cats were somewhere else. So, by prospecting with lighter gear, Gray and Elliot knew their hole of choice about six miles west of Jaquith's Boat Landing at Vermillion, held at least one huge fish.

The day they caught the big fish, Charlie Gray came by Elliot's shop early. He suggested that the mist made it an ideal day. Elliot didn't want to fish. Gray convinced him to play hooky. So they launched their barge from the old wildlife landing west of Vermillion and chugged downstream to a deep hole in the main channel of the Missouri. Elliot said, "We anchored just below a sandbar near what's now Clay County Park and set our baits—we only had a small carp that we cut into chunks—in about 30 feet of water."

When they pulled into their favorite hole about six in the evening, they had a good idea about records, as Elliot said, because "a friend had just caught the 94½-pound record. That sure didn't last long!" They were hopeful because Charlie Gray had caught a 72-pound cat from the water, and he thought that there might be another in this untamed section of the river.

After they set out their big rods in holders, they started to fish away from the hole with spinning gear for saugers, a favorite dinner fish. As Elliot remembers it, "I had my camo rain suit on because it was still misty, and I was looking the wrong way when the fish hit. Charlie yelled 'Fish on!'" It hadn't been long at all; they had been on the hole for less than 30 minutes.

When Elliot grabbed his sturdy rod, its tip was already submerged. He could feel the fish surge off as he struggled to haul the rod out of the holder. Then, he set himself, and "banged the hook in as hard as he could manage."

The fish smoothly, if somewhat slowly, raced off. Elliot

braced himself on the side of the barge and held on. Gray cleared his line, moved gear out of Elliot's way, and freed his big homemade net. Elliot said, "I told him to put the net away. This one was going to take awhile."

By the time the first run stopped, Elliot could see the spool through his last layer or two of 80-pound-test line. Then, the fight settled down into a slugging match. Elliot would pull and pump, but even with 80-pound-test line, the catfish would turn sideways, then bank away from the boat and sail downstream with the help of the current. Only the length of the hole, and the big cat's desire to stay in deep water, kept the fight within the 100-yard capacity of Elliot's reel.

Even so, Gray considered firing up the engine and, twice had to clear the anchor so the big fish wouldn't snag it. It took over 40 minutes to haul the big cat near the boat. The big fish broke water about 20 yards out. As Elliot remembers it, "When the cat rolled, Charlie yelled, 'You got a 100-pounder!' Boy, did I get excited," Elliot said, "I knew the world record was only 94½ pounds."

Finally, they saw a tail through the muddy water. Then, the back appeared "as broad as a big dog's." The massive head still strained downward. Gray poised his net. Then, with a doubtful look at the size of Elliot's monster catfish, submerged the net in the current. Elliot steered the tiring cat over the poised net. As its body brushed the mesh, the big fish dived. Its head hit the mesh. It took both Elliot and Gray to lift the catfish into the boat. Its body overlapped the net even when bent double, causing the net to sag out of shape.

They moved the fish into the cabin on the barge. Elliot said, "It had scars all over its mouth and head. It had to be the ugliest fish I'd ever seen. Still, it didn't seem nearly as wet and uncomfortable as I felt before the fish hit."

A rest, a cool drink, some speculation on the size of the fish and, with fishing time left, Gray and Elliot stayed out on the river. Elliot said, "It was six hours or more before we weighed the fish at a certified scale at the local dairy." South Dakota fisheries experts report that, "It was certain to have weighed more than 100 pounds when fresh. It's amazing that Elliot and Gray didn't come in right away."

The reason for their lack of surprise may have been the 90-,

72- and 55-pound fish they had taken that year and the "over 650" catfish above 65 pounds Gray had caught as he perfected techniques and refined his approach.

"Charlie never did catch a record-book fish," Elliot explained, the regret plainly in his voice.

He continued, "I wonder how many other fishermen do the work only to see someone else set the record. It's a shame really. These days, with the river way down because of dams and agricultural needs, the average catfish size has dropped so much you don't have to worry about records. I wish Charlie had his name somewhere. I've got both the National Fresh Water Fishing Hall of Fame and the International Game Fish Association records. It's too bad he couldn't have shared these. I never would have landed the fish without his help. Never would have got started fishing cats if it hadn't been for him, either."

When questioned about his record fish, Elliot said, "I had it mounted. That seemed a shame. It was such a homely fish. I didn't even want to hang it in the basement." So a friend displayed the fish in a bar until 1965. The fish looked worse every year. Then the bar burned down. When told that fiberglass replicas were available, Elliot responded, "Why would anyone want to display something as ugly as that?"

Clearly, Elliot looks ahead, not back. Now 83 years old, and married 54 years, he drives his 26-foot Airstream from eastern South Dakota to British Columbia every year for a two- or three-month stay. "Salmon do fight better than catfish," he said, "but I've only caught salmon up to 33 pounds. I often wonder what a 97-pound salmon would feel like.

"It took a heap of luck to catch that fish. There were a lot of snags—trees, snags, cables and barrels on the barge—it was lucky." However, turning up with the expert who had caught more catfish that anyone, securing saltwater gear in the middle of the country, and being able to slug it out with such a heavyweight seems far more than luck!

Complete Angler's Library

9

Mike Rodgers' Monster Flathead

Sometimes, you can improve your fishing chances. Sometimes, it helps to be plain lucky. Mike Rodgers improved his chances with crappie in Lewisville Lake, a mature impoundment with sometimes sparse cover, by sinking his own private artificial reef of Christmas trees early in 1982. By March, crappie moved into feed. Rodgers had the ideal outfit for crappie—a small Mitchell spinning reel filled with 12-pound test line, light Berkley rod and a crappie-size hook lightly weighted to take a live minnow down to the tinsel-draped branches below. Crappie fishing seemed a bit slow that day. Then, Rodgers had a light bite and set the hook. "The fish took off like a submarine," he said.

Rodgers, then a Lewisville area resident and his buddy, Don Teeple from Oklahoma, had hooked a lot bigger fish than either of them expected. They knew at once it was a monster catfish. Only catfish chug off a spool of line with a slow, steady pace. For a moment, Rodgers considered breaking off the fish so he could get back to crappie fishing. Then, he flipped open the bale of his spinning reel so the fish could run as he tried to plug in his electric trolling motor. His buddy, Don, got the anchor up.

According to Rodgers' statements in Mike McDonald's Dallas Times Herald column of May 28, 1982, "It was like a fire drill. I got the trolling motor hooked up only out of sheer panic. Away we went. We did some figure-eights, circles—it was a regular Ice Capades. The fish would stop and sound on me, I guess trying to dig into the mud. Bubbles would come up. I thought maybe I hooked a skin diver.

"My arm was about to give out. It felt like Jell-O. It got so I didn't care. I said to myself, 'You're never going to see this fish.' When I said to Don, 'Maybe we should cut the line.' Don said, 'You cut that line, and I'll cut your throat.'"

Don Teeple said it took 35 minutes for the fish to roll at the boat. Teeple reached gingerly for the fish; its head looked big enough to swallow his entire arm. The giant flathead chugged away. Ten more minutes went by. Rodgers wondered if the line would hold. Teeple wondered how he would grab the huge cat.

When the cat came near the boat again and its huge head broke the water, Teeple said, "Mike, we need a bigger net." Teeple was right. After several attempts, Teeple grabbed the cat's tail; Rodgers hauled on the head. On the first haul, the catfish balanced on the gunwale. A second haul sent it thumping into the bow of the boat. Teeple and Rodgers moved back to the boat's stern out of range of the big cat's mighty mouth.

It took 90 minutes to get the huge fish to a set of beef scales. It probably lost a couple of pounds to dehydration, and might have topped 100 pounds. After weighing the fish and a photo session, Teeple and Rodgers field dressed the huge catfish. Rodgers said, "When we opened it up, I expected hubcaps and license plates to fall out." The fish weighed in at 91 pounds, 4 ounces. They saved the head for mounting and cut up the rest of the fish with a butcher's bandsaw. Rodgers regrets not keeping the fish alive. "I was in such a daze, I let everybody do my thinking for me," he said, "I should have kept it and taken it to the Dallas Aquarium at Fair Park."

It took some time for Rodgers to calm down. "Right after I caught the fish," he said, "I was so high I couldn't sleep for about a week. After a while, I was getting everything under control, but after the news release from the state and all the phone calls I'm hyper again."

The joke here, for the dozens of Lewisville Lake catfish specialists, is that Rodgers still doesn't consider himself a catfisherman. "Catfisherman go out for the meat," he said. "I like to watch fish dance on the water. I love to eat fish, but I like the sport of catching them on rod and reel." So much for

A bystander poses with the 99-pound flathead catfish taken from Lake Livingston in Texas. The only "catch" to this catch is that the fish was taken on a trotline which is legal in that state, but disqualifies it for national recognition.

the idea of fishing specialization when taking catfish!

Lewisville Lake's Lunker Cats

Lewisville Lake, a 23,280-acre reservoir north of Dallas is one of those special waters that, like Florida's Merritt Pond for shellcrackers, offers ideal conditions for flathead catfish. Bobby Farquhar, a biologist with the Texas Parks and Wildlife Department, said, "Shallow, turbid reservoirs with plenty of food for both large and small catfish aren't common in Texas. Lewisville is perfect. It's got shad and bass for big catfish to eat and insects for small fish. It's the best catfish lake in Texas."

Farquhar continued, "April action around the riprap on the dam and bridges peaks when catfish gobble gar eggs. Otherwise, deep water near the dam is the choice. Lewisville may offer the most comfortable fishing in Texas, too! An air-conditioned fishing barge suits summer fishermen when it's hot and humid."

Only In Texas

Texans do look at catfish differently. They recognize both rod and reel and unrestricted records, and residents seem to practice some rather unconventional techniques. For example, William Stephens of Lewisville once held the IGFA record with a 98-pound flathead caught out of the Lake Lewisville spillway on June 2, 1986. For a period, this fish held the world all-tackle record. Then, when Stephens was discussing his record with a writer from *the In Fisherman* who was doing a book on catfish, Stephens admitted that he had snagged the fish. This is both a legal and accepted practice in Texas and some other states. When the writer asked, "How could the fish be the record. You can't snag IGFA or NFWFHF records?" Stephens immediately responded, "I didn't know that. We better tell them right away." Stephens did. Both bodies rescinded Stephens' record.

That's the problem with flathead catfish. Like Rodney Dangerfield, they get no respect and, for many, anything goes with gear and techniques. If more fishermen considered them as one of the few heavy tackle challenges in freshwater, they might be better treated. Anything that large, and that old, deserves that!

=====10=====
Black Bullhead—Catfish Confusion

Black bullhead confusion starts with two records. The IGFA lists Kani Evans' 8-pound bullhead caught in 1951 from Lake Waccabuc, New York. The NFWFHF lists Charles Taylor's 8-pound, 15-ounce fish caught from Sturgis Pond, Michigan, in 1987. New York state records do not list the Evans bullhead; they cite a 2-pound, 8-ounce tiddler instead. One of their biologists insists the Evans fish is misidentified. The IGFA, it must be noted, really didn't identify this fish. It was grandfathered-in with the old *Field & Stream* records when IGFA took over that program.

The State of Michigan didn't list the record until the family opened the pond up to the public. Even then state record-keepers didn't know about the fish until called for an interview during the preparation of this book. One of their biologists, however, did certify the Taylor record as a black bullhead. IGFA did not agree.

Black bullheads obviously are subject to species confusion of all sorts. So while some think the Evans record wasn't properly identified, and the Taylor record should be allowed, readers can make up their own minds. Here are the facts.

The Evans Effort
Nobody seems to know about this fish, aside from the fact it came from a 139-acre lake in suburban Westchester County in 1951 and won the *Field & Stream* contest that year.

A New York Fisheries biologist said, "We don't even list that as a state record. There are at least a couple of things wrong with that record. To start, black bullheads are not native to that area. The fish seems too big for a brown or yellow, too. Of course, bullheads are hard for the layman to identify. It's my understanding that the old *Field & Stream* rules were not that strict on species identification."

He continued, "If I had to guess, I'd say it was probably a white catfish." Such absent evidence to the contrary, seems a reasonable standard. Michael Leech, an IGFA official, said, "We are trying to work through some of the old records grandfathered in, but you have to be careful, it takes time. And, frankly, the black bullhead record has a fairly low priority."

There seems little chance to check this record. The boat livery where the fish was probably weighed has been closed for years. Inquiries at local tackle shops were fruitless.

The Backyard Bullhead

Charles Taylor's father dug his pond by the house in 1974. For years, the family fished nearby lakes in St. Joseph County and dumped the small fish they caught into their pond. Charles' father says, "I assume the record was one of four 'bullheads' I caught in 1974 and put in the pond. With all the problems with the record I wish we'd eaten the fish."

Charles was 14 years old in the summer of 1987 when he caught the fish. He says, "We used to fish the pond a lot in the summer. Sometimes we caught bass. Sometimes we caught panfish. That afternoon we were trying for bass with live frogs we'd snagged, then hooked with a No. 2 hook. I had a little Shimano reel and a 6-foot rod. It worked great for the kind of fish we usually caught. It was about dark. I let the frog swim around off the bank. Then, the line started to move out. When I set the hook, I thought I had a big, old bass. The pond is black water so you can't see fish when you hook them so I wasn't sure. After about 10 minutes, I saw some white belly. I was sure it was a big bass."

Charles sent his cousin, Jason Harper, then 13 years old, running back to the farm for help and a bigger net. They had tried to net the fish from the bank "two or three times," but the

This 8-pound, 15½-ounce NFWFHF record black bullhead was caught by Charles M. Taylor in Sturgis Pond in Michigan in August, 1987.

light rod and line couldn't bring it in close enough. Then, Charles' father showed up to help. Charles said, "My dad almost fell into the water twice." Taylor's father paddled a small boat out onto the pond and tried to net the fish again. That didn't work either. He finally got back on the bank and netted the fish. It certainly wasn't a bass! It was 26 inches long and properly weighed 8 pounds, 15½ ounces.

Katherine Grimm, a Michigan fisheries habitat biologist, examined the fish and certified it as a black bullhead on August 21, 1987. Charles' father said, "It's still hanging in Bart's Bait on US 12W in Sturgis. But it won't be there long, the mount is falling apart."

Charles, with the help of his father and grandfather, forwarded his paperwork, line samples and photos to IGFA,

NFWFHF and the State of Michigan for certification. Charles' grandfather said, "IGFA refused the record based on species identification. According to them the fish was a catfish, not a bullhead."

Charles and his father tried for IGFA certification for a year and a half, but IGFA refused the record. Since only the IGFA ruling counted, Charles missed out on the $10,000 Trilene prize money awarded for new world records at the time.

Bob Kutz, the founder of the NFWFHF, requested further line samples before he finally granted both line class and all-tackle records. Charles holds one of the Hall's official recognition certificates that commemorate a world record angling achievement.

The State of Michigan first refused both the state record and one of their Master Angler awards. Michigan officials said, "The pond was private, and there had to be public access for record qualification." Only after Charles' grandfather signed a statement that he would allow public fishing by request, was the Michigan state record and master angler award granted.

How Much Bull In Your Bullhead?

So the question remains, which of these "records" is really a black bullhead? If you accept the word of the New York fisheries expert about "size unlikely" it seems almost certain that the Evans fish was misidentified. With the Taylor fish, you have the identification of a fisheries biologist, and a skin mount to rely on. So can you really say, like the New York fisheries biologist that, "Black Bullheads simply don't get that big." Given the other records for black bullheads, the record size seems possible, if very uncommon. Given the smaller records for the other bullhead species, if Charles Taylor's fish was in fact a bullhead, the odds are extremely good that it was a black bullhead rather than a brown or yellow.

However, misidentifications remain a problem with scaleless fish that all potential record-setters must realize. Brown, black, yellow and flathead bullheads come in all colors and can be confused with blue, channel, white and flathead catfish at various stages. Catfish are all scaleless; they all have a single dorsal fin and an adipose fin, strong spines in the dorsal and pectoral fins, and whisker-like sensory barbels on their upper and lower jaws. The head and mouth of all of these fish is broad, and the eyes always small.

There is, absent a photo, a mounted specimen, or the certification of a fisheries expert, no easy way to determine the species of Evans' fish. Applying the Occam's Razor's test, i.e. the simplest solution—in this case misidentification—as the most likely, Evans' fish was probably a catfish.

Such is not the case with Charles Taylor's fish. Field marks for the various bullheads and likely catfish are not that confusing for a trained fisheries biologist even though the photo of Charles Taylor and his fish, like many record photos, does present a problem. It's impossible to see if the tail has the deep fork characteristic of the channel catfish. However, channel catfish have 24 to 30 rays on their rounded anal fin. Black bullheads have 17 to 21 rays. Examination of the photo with a strong lens suggests the number of rays does not exceed 20. This alone would rule out channel and blue catfish. We can eliminate the flat bullhead because of its southern range and small size.

What's left are brown and yellow bullheads and white catfish. The mounted Taylor fish does not have the strong barbs characteristic of brown bullheads. Its ray count is not high enough for yellow bullheads, and it lacks the whitish lower barbels characteristic of this species. So the sole remaining candidate is a white catfish. It has the same approximate number of rays as the black bullhead, but its anal fin is more rounded and, in most cases, smaller. However, white catfish sides have no markings, and dim markings seem apparent on the rather poor snapshots of Charles Taylor's fish.

Most important of all, we have the testimony and, on the application, the signature of a trained fisheries biologist who certified the fish as a black bullhead.

It's also worth pointing out that other IGFA and NFWFHF black bullhead records are identical and large enough to suggest that the maximum weights in fisheries biology literature, perhaps the basis of the New York fisheries biologist's statement, may be too low. Just on a size basis, all of the bullheads and blue, white, channel and flathead catfish are possibilities to be eliminated.

Given these records, all carefully identified by both

record-granting bodies, it seems likely that, first, an 8-pound 15-ounce black bullhead is possible and, second, the Taylor record, since it was certified by a qualified fisheries biologist, should be the all-tackle black bullhead world record unless there were problems other than species identification.

Mike Leech, at IGFA, said, "We always state the reason in a letter when we turn down a record application." Such a letter was not part of Charles Taylor's information package on which this chapter is based. When asked, Charles Taylor's father did not remember any IGFA letter. IGFA has sent their correspondence to a warehouse. So readers can make up their own minds, perhaps with a trip to Bart's Bait at Sturgis, Michigan, before that skin mount falls off the wall!

=====11=====

Largest Freshwater Fish

Sturgeon have always been royal fish. It wasn't until February, 1971, that the British House of Lords took the sovereign's entitlement of all sturgeon in English waters away from the king. So it seems suitably "all-American" that the record 468-pound white sturgeon was caught by a union plumber on his day off. Joey Pallotta will even take you fishing. He skippers the party boat Captain K for Crockett Sportfishing out of Crockett, California, on weekends. He specializes in sturgeon, but you won't break his record. California, like other states with white sturgeon, has changed the rules. Today, you can either catch and release in states like Idaho, or keep fish that are between 44 and 72 inches, like California. So his "super sturgeon" record seems safe.

Pallotta's Record

Pallotta, as he remembers back to July 9, 1983, "really expected to catch a record sturgeon eventually. I had decent depthfinders and had pinpointed the ledge and underwater cave where I thought big sturgeon hid on incoming tides."

Rumors of big fish abounded in the strait that connects the saltwater of San Francisco and San Pablo bays with the brackish California Delta. Fishing pressure is extremely heavy there during seasons when striped bass, salmon and steelhead migrate inland. Shad and a number of other species use this windy passage of constricted waters, too. Many locals hooked and,

Largest Freshwater Fish   81 after seconds, minutes or hours of suffering the heavy pull of unseen fish, broken off a monster that some called "Tugboat Charlie."

Pallotta is certain he didn't catch "Tugboat Charlie."

"A friend whom I trust was out in a 16-foot skiff," as Pallotta recalls it. "He hooked a big fish and got up in the bow to play it after they dumped the anchor. He got too close to the fish and, with his rod out over the bow, saw the fish's head at the same moment the sturgeon's tail hit their outboard hard enough to knock the lower unit out of the water. An 18-foot-long fish like that could weigh a ton."

One reason bigger sturgeon haven't been caught since they stopped fishing for them with set lines hauled in with teams of horses is congestion. A number of yacht harbors, marinas and Martinez, Benicia and Crockett add to the boater's bumper car crowds in the strait. Deal in tankers heading to or from the Shell oil refinery, container ships bound inland to Stockton or Sacramento, nuclear submarines bound for the sub base in Vallejo and the usual assortment of sailboats and casual summer boaters and you know why Pallotta had his anchor buoyed for a quick release.

"Sturgeon fishing is a lot more relaxing than most methods for people that work hard," Pallotta said. "You rig up with a heavy reel and line, bait with grass shrimp and wait, and wait and wait. But you'd better have heavy gear. People rigged for stripers or flounders don't have a chance with light gear in strong currents dodging heavy boat traffic."

That day Pallotta had a heavy Fenwick reel and a Daiwa 50H reel filled with all the 60-pound, IGFA-rated Stren he could jam on. Nearly a pound of lead held his grass shrimp clump, rigged on 6/0 hooks to the 68-foot-deep bottom off Benicia's 9th Street. Pallotta called his rig "sort of an accident." He had planned to rig for stripers out at the center pier of the Carquinez Bridge, but it was too windy and there were too many boats. So he moved back away from San Pablo Bay.

Pallotta and his girlfriend enjoyed lunch and were just about dozing as they worked on their suntans that warm afternoon after a hard week's work. Although it isn't usual in the strait, it was fairly calm and passing sailboats barely ghosted by. Suddenly, over his girl friend's shoulder, Pallotta saw that the

Joey Pallotta's 468-pound white sturgeon is a world-record catch that will remain unchallenged because of rule changes on the taking of white sturgeon. But Pallotta's convinced there are even larger sturgeon where this one was taken.

tip of his rod was being pulled nearly into the water.

He jumped up and stroked hard to set the hook. For an instant, he thought he had snagged bottom. Then, his line went slack. Pallotta reeled fast, half convinced he had lost the fish. Then, the huge fish surged out of the water just 50 yards from the boat. It was so heavy it couldn't jump all of the way out of the water, but it cleared the brown brackish surface with its head, shook its gills, slammed back in the water and took off for the Carquinez Bridge. The sound, according to Pallotta, "was like someone had dumped a bathtub into the water. Awesome!"

There were lots of witnesses. A sailboat load of Pallotta's friends screamed advice and instructions as he fought the fish, then the boat headed toward Dowrellio's Yacht Harbor and

Vallejo to spread the word about the fish that had Pallotta. The huge sturgeon towed Pallotta's 18-foot-long runabout toward the Carquinez Bridge, then back toward the Benicia Marina as the tide topped, then turned. Other fishermen moved in to gawk. Pallotta yelled at them to stay back. Fortunately, friends turned up in a skiff to keep spectators at a fair distance.

Pallotta hauled hard on the fish. He tried to vary the angle so he always pulled to the side. The deep water helped, as he was able to shorten down the line and keep the big fish off bottom and away from snags. He also managed to keep the huge sturgeon from rolling up in the leader, a favorite tactic of this monster fish.

It took five hours and 30 minutes before Pallotta, now almost exhausted, could jam a rope through the sturgeon's gills and another around its tail. Then, it took another half hour to haul the massive fish back to the dock and to a certified scale. Pallotta, who had planned on setting the record and knew the importance of the proper procedures, called the California Department of Fish and Game. They arrived almost immediately and certified the fish as a white sturgeon.

Pallotta's sturgeon weighed 468 pounds. It's mounted and displayed at the Crockett Museum. A huge photo of the fish can be seen in the Guinness World Record Museum in San Francisco. Pallotta sent the required line samples to NFWFHF and IGFA. So Pallotta's fish holds both all-tackle records, the IGFA 80-pound-test line class record, the NFWFHF 60-pound-test line class record and the California state record. However, he said, "the best thing about the record was the chance it gave me to become a party boat skipper and get paid to spend my weekends and time off out on the water."

It's even better for Pallotta that the California regulation for sturgeon changed after his catch. Bigger sturgeon swim in the murky waters of the Carquinez Strait, in San Pablo Bay and around the hulls of the Mothball Fleet just inland from the Martinez Bridge. Old records out of nearby Point San Pablo show sturgeon weights pushing 2,000 pounds. These were taken with ropes or nets and hauled out on the bank with horses.

Today, only San Pablo Bay offers a realistic chance at Pallotta's record with the fairly lightweight gear favored by San Francisco Bay anglers. So, it's unlikely that a bigger sturgeon than Pallotta's would come from the Carquinez Strait except at dead low or high tide. The waters rush through this constricted waterway with so much force you can sit on the bank at Dillon's Point and still troll a striper plug in the current. Hook a sturgeon there, follow it and you may end up at Sausalito nearly 10 miles down bay!

The Mothball Fleet, "decommissioned" Navy ships anchored out in long gray rows at the delta end of the strait, also produce "temporary custody" of huge sturgeon that quickly cut lines on rusty mooring wires. If a bigger sturgeon bites and could be played to the boat, it's most likely to be found in the shallow waters of San Pablo Bay where, in days when sturgeon were illegal to keep, fishermen would quickly break them off.

Pallotta expects to hook, play and land a bigger fish from San Pablo Bay off his party boat, but its weight will have to be "guesstimated."

Sturgeon Slot Limits

It's a good thing sturgeon now enjoy the shelter from over-harvest produced by slot limits! These mighty, prehistoric fish certainly deserve special protection for their age, their bulk, their delicious flesh and their wonderful eggs (the raw material for caviar). Twice in the past, without slot limit protection, California sturgeon were fished almost to extinction.

Today's slot limits are needed because sturgeon grow slowly to reproductive age. Biologists try to set regulations so fish can spawn at least once before they are caught and then, because the biggest fish are almost always females, protect the most prolific egg layers.

California goes a bit further than most states with a Russian emigre fisheries expert at the University of California, Davis which now raises and releases small sturgeon. Until recently, hatchery white sturgeon were considered impossible to stock in the United States."

Size And Age Records

Sturgeon stocked today may see the 22nd Century, because sturgeon may live 150 to 175 years. The oldest age sample, based on a pectoral fin ring count, is 82 years. Size estimates vary as well. Some old records claim 2,000 pounds. Most of these fish had to be cut up into pieces in order to be weighed on grain scales.

A well-authenticated specimen 12½ feet long and weighing 1,285 pounds was taken in 1912, 125 miles up the Columbia River near Vancouver, Washington, when it became tangled in a gill net. The fish held 125 pounds of eggs, verifying the theory that larger fish yield more eggs.

An even larger sturgeon was reported from the Fraser River in British Columbia some 50 years ago. It measured almost 20 feet in length, was nearly a century old and strained the scales at 1,832 pounds. Recent reports mention 500- to 800-pound fish from the Lillooet area of the Fraser River. In B.C., locals use 35- to 80-pound test line, ocean rods and peculiar single action "knuckle duster" reels that only hold 170 or so yards of line, a popular practice with fishermen who mooch salmon.

According to British Columbia Tourism, "There seems little doubt that a world-record IGFA sturgeon will be taken soon from the lower Fraser River." Skeptics might suggest that locals invest in a big Fin-Nor or Penn reel with star drags at the minimum, and a billfish drag system. The local guides and fisheries experts have set up a unique sling weighing system. This allows fish to be towed to the weighing station, weighed to meet IGFA and NFWFHF standards, photographed and released to breed. Such a system might work for California, too.

12

Earning Lake Sturgeon Record

Fortunately, lake sturgeon only swim in the waters of conservative Canada and the Midwest. The mind boggles at the behavior of hyper New Yorkers like Montauk surf casters exposed to such a "piscatorial high" trip; it reels at the image of "Hey, Dude" Los Angeles fishermen chasing fish bigger than surfers' boards down concrete-lined riverbeds—assuming, of course, that the rivers still had water. Still, sturgeon do have a "California" image with their tan, brown or golden scaleless smooth skin stretched around a sleek body. Lake sturgeon make fishermen as crazy as a teenager's hormones at a California bikini beach.

Sturgeon records may be even more crazed. Photos of fish over 200 pounds exist, 300-pound fish were taken from Lake Superior and Lake Michigan, and a number of large fish have been speared over decoys suspended under holes in the ice at Wisconsin's Lake Winnebago. The speared Michigan-record fish ran 193 pounds.

Uncharitable types suggest that only the mad would hunker down in a dark hut and twiddle a weighted wooden fish through a coffin-size hole to attract sturgeon that cautiously move in to inspect a decoy and are then speared as they move away. Saner souls might question the desire to be confined in a small hut holding onto one end of a long stick with a thrashing monster on the other. Compared to this, rod-and-reel types seem staid and solid vestrymen.

Sturgeon big enough for Loch Ness may fin Great Lakes waters. Scale and other tests show a slow sturgeon growth rate, but a maximum lifespan of 150 years. Most of these giants are, by their very size, hook-proof against usual tackle and techniques.

Unfortunately, sturgeon spawning in shallow waters are exposed to spearing, roping, netting, shooting and other forms of molestation even outside the few states—the Dakotas, Minnesota, Wisconsin and Michigan—where lake sturgeon are legal species.

These huge fish simply don't practice secret sex. When sturgeon spawn in riffles and rapids in May and June they make more noise than NFL linebackers blasting backs on crossing patterns. Males often cruise with tails and snouts out of the water. The larger females—all really big lake sturgeon are female—are quite vulnerable at this time. Add the price of sturgeon meat, with its exquisite veal texture. Consider the "if you have to ask, you can't afford it" price sturgeon caviar fetches, and it's easy to see why poaching is a major threat.

Even rod-and-reel records are suspect. Several early record fish proved to be netted. A recent record fish turned out to be reeled in by two fishermen. Supposedly, it even sported rope burns. Questions arose about water clarity where the catch was claimed. These also suggested roping, and might have secured the fish until the season opened. When the local fish and game officials called to inspect after rumors of suspicious circumstances surfaced, the fishermen who caught the fish reported unknown parties had stolen the fish from the garage freezer. Even though substantial rewards were offered, the "mystery" sturgeon submerged forever. It only surfaces as a local joke.

The Planner's Record

Jim DeOtis's record fish shines against this rather murky background. It's an exceptional example of good planning, excellent execution, exact attention to rules, and considerable luck. DeOtis isn't your typical casual outdoorsman who lucks into a record fish. He works summers at camps as a naturalist and survival expert, traps in the fall and works for a fur company in the winter. In between, he camps alone in the wilderness.

James Michael DeOtis stands beside the 92-pound, 4-ounce lake sturgeon that he caught in Minnesota's Kettle River. The fish is the all-tackle record for both IGFA and NFWFHF.

Earning Lake Sturgeon Record

His favorite camping spot where he now sets up camp, a two-mile kayak paddle down the Kettle River from road access, is on a large hole where DeOtis had seen a number of large sturgeon jump. He had caught a number of sturgeon in the 3- to 50-pound range, but none were as large as his record. Otherwise, he might have brought heavier gear than the medium-weight Berkley rod he used to cast a No. 2 Eagle Claw hook baited with a worm and the Garcia Mitchell 900 reel he had filled with 15-pound-test Berkley line.

DeOtis had kayaked into the perfect record setting. The Kettle, a tributary of the St. Croix River, was the first, and arguably the finest, "wild and scenic" river in Minnesota. It runs clear and cold between walls of sumac, wild roses and ferns about an hour's drive north of Minneapolis.

"I probably have 20 months of solo camping on the Kettle during the last five or six years," DeOtis said. "I like the Kettle because it's the closest wilderness to the Twin Cities, and great for survival-type camping."

Just at dusk the night of September 11, 1986, DeOtis pitched his worm bait into the head of the hole where the river widened between its overgrown banks. He braced the rod on a forked stick, wired it in place and attached a bell. Then, before he retired to his tent to work on a book he was putting together on edible plants and survival techniques, he set a number of mouse traps outside his nearby supply tent, so mice wouldn't gnaw their way into his food.

After a couple of traps snapped, DeOtis, now stripped down to underwear and moccasins, grabbed a small flashlight and headed out to empty and reset traps. Suddenly, the rod's bell clattered. DeOtis raced to the rod, and cranked in slack, but felt nothing. The rodtip didn't even twitch. So DeOtis reset his traps and headed back to his sleeping tent. "It was a bit cool standing there in my moccasins and underwear," he said. "And they kept announcing on the news to look at the northern lights."

Only when DeOtis looked back toward the river did he notice his rod was bent. He ran to the rod and set the hook, but nothing happened.

"At first it was like hauling in a log," DeOtis said. "Then, the log tore off downstream. I couldn't follow the fish very far.

The shore cover was too thick. I was so afraid I'd run out of line that I dragged my kayak down to the river so I could attempt to follow the fish in the kayak if necessary.

"I didn't have any control at all," he said. "The fish ran all over the place. It was a miracle that it didn't break me off on a snag. Then, I ran out of hands and ended up holding my flashlight in my mouth."

After the first hard runs, DeOtis hit on a plan. He'd reel in against the line—there was never slack—as he moved downstream 25 to 30 feet to the edge of impassable timber. Then, using his fingers on the spool to increase the drag, he slowly backed upstream. Again and again over the next two hours, DeOtis repeated this pattern. He gained line, and confidence enough so, as his flashlight dimmed, he was able to edge away from the water to his tent in order to get a larger flashlight and his pants.

Then, as the long, dark shape of the sturgeon finned just out of reach, DeOtis kicked off his moccasins and waded in. He knew the giant fish would spook when handled. "The first couple of times I touched the fish I intended to scare it," he said. The fish surged away, then, ever so slowly, returned. The third time he pumped the fish back he was able to grab the small of the tail with one hand and jerk his prize up on the bank. He dropped his rod, grabbed the fish with both hands and hauled it 6 feet away from the water.

"I let go of the fish, as I had to take a couple of steps to grab a rope," DeOtis said. "Instead of trying to get back in the water, the fish slowly raised and turned its head toward me and repeatedly, viciously, swung its tail at me.

"I hopped on its back and started wrestling the fish, trying to turn it over so I could stick a rope in through its gills and out its mouth. It took about five minutes to do it, but I got a rope through, knotted it about 20 times and then ran another rope through the other gill, just to be on the safe side. I picked out a very large tree next to the shore and attached both ropes to the tree. Then, I put the fish back in the water. Only then could I relax, but I was so excited I kept getting up every hour or so to check that the fish was still roped.

"The next morning I untied the ropes from the tree and went to attach the fish to my kayak so I could paddle up the

Jim DeOtis holds the framed certificate and replica of his catch which bears testimony to his accomplishment in landing the record sturgeon.

river to my car. The fish blasted off downstream. I pulled, fought and struggled. It was no use. I got dragged right into the river. I was nearly in over my head before the fish gave up and I could secure it to my kayak for the trip to the scales."

It took DeOtis several hours to paddle his kayak back upstream against the current with the huge live sturgeon lunging this way and that on the end of its rope. DeOtis could not kill the fish by bashing it on the head because he knew any damage might suggest the fish was clubbed or otherwise illegally taken and would be disqualified.

Exhausted after getting up through the night to check his fish, and by the tough paddle upstream against the Kettle's current and the sturgeon's attempts to break free, DeOtis dragged the fish to his car. He said, "I still feel bad that the fish eventually suffocated in the truck. But I couldn't bash it. There had been too many stories about clubbed sturgeon."

It was only a short drive to nearby Hinckley, Minnesota, and the Department of Natural Resources (DNR) office. DNR officials quickly determined the old Minnesota lake sturgeon record, set on the St. Croix River, was 91 pounds. Unfortunately, they didn't have a scale. So as word got round and a crowd gathered, everyone headed over to the local Super Valu grocery store where DNR officers weighed and witnessed the fish. Then, DeOtis, aware of the "fine print," noticed that the Super Valu scale had not been certified within the last year as the IGFA standards require. One gets the feeling that DeOtis had read the fine print very carefully indeed on slow nights in his camp on the river!

A few calls turned up a currently certified scale nearby in Hinckley. In the meantime, helpful DNR officers found a stock tank, stuck it on a truck, filled it with water, and used it to transport the fish to its legal weighing spot. The sturgeon ran a record 92 pounds, 4 ounces with a 69-inch length and a 30-inch girth.

At this point, DeOtis clearly had the new Minnesota lake sturgeon record. He also applied to IGFA and NFWFHF for certification. DeOtis had selected 15-pound-test line because the IGFA record in that class was lower than that in the 12-pound test class. Unfortunately, the IGFA test found the sample testing at 12 pounds and it refused a line test record for 12-pound test because the existing 12-pound test record was a 168-pound white sturgeon—IGFA only split white and lake sturgeon classes three years later. The NFWFHF gave DeOtis its all-tackle and 15-pound line test records based on their line tests.

DeOtis feels the difference between the IGFA 12-pound test line rating and the NFWFHF 15-pound-test line rating came because he sent the first section of line off his reel to IGFA. That section was abraded by his sturgeon during the long fight. His abraded line and the IGFA-delayed split of sturgeon records cost DeOtis his chance at the $1,000 Berkley Trilene prize offered for IGFA line class records caught on their line.

This doesn't seem to bother DeOtis. He still kayaks and camps alone on the Kettle. He still fishes and traps his favorite waters, and he still holds the records he sought. His 15-pound line class record may stand for decades, but his all-tackle records seem at risk.

Perspectives

The Michigan state record fish mounted in the state's tourism office weighed 193 pounds when it was speared through the ice by Joe Maka on February 16, 1974. Even larger records of 212-, 220-, 236- and 275-pound lake sturgeon are noted by Canadian biologists. Since improved electronics make it easier to locate the few monster sturgeon that have survived from a once-flourishing Great Lakes fishery, and a growing number of fishermen seek them out with gear stout enough to drag these massive fish off bottom, we may see the all-tackle record head north to Canada.

However, this kind of high-tech, low-technique approach clearly does not interest Jim DeOtis. He hasn't even kept his mounted fish that, considering DeOtis's favorite footwear, appropriately hangs on the wall at the Moccasin Bar in Hayward, Wisconsin, near the National Fresh Water Fishing Hall of Fame. Jim DeOtis is into more elemental things—like sporting tackle and wrestling a fish that's only an inch shorter than his 5-foot, 10-inch body—and all this miles from nowhere.

=======13=======

Kings Of The Kenai

laska's Kenai River, in its 85 miles of glacial
silt-clouded water, must be the most popular trophy
chinook salmon fishery in the world. No place else
can you find so many kings, the Alaskan term for
chinook salmon that anglers in other areas respectfully call
"spring salmon or tyee." No place else concentrates so many
huge fish in such a small area so convenient to transportation,
lodging and guide services. As a result, Alaskan locals and
"lower 48" visitors invest over 125,000 man-days of fishing.
This means plenty of competition for the biggest salmon.

Locals, like Lester Anderson, and guided fishermen do have
an advantage. In 1985, Anderson used his knowledge of the
special demands of the Kenai kings to take a 97-pound, 4-ounce
monster. Had Anderson weighed it immediately, it might have
topped the 100-pound mark. Visitors who want to better their
feat are well-advised to book guided trips, because the Kenai
River bites. The heavy flows that evolve monster-size salmon
also upset boats and can drown fishermen unfamiliar with
Alaskan rivers.

Gearing Up With Lester Anderson

Anderson, then the owner of the Ford dealership in nearby
Soldatna, had solved the special problems fishermen face when
trying to lure salmon in big rivers with poor visibility due to
glacial silt, and the bigger problems of trying to land huge fish

in the heavy water of these Alaskan rivers.

"Visitors who don't go with guides generally don't have the right gear," Anderson said. "I used a big Garcia spinning reel with top-quality, 25-pound-test line and a special rod my buddy Clarence Wait made. Most 'lower 48' rods don't have enough backbone for Kenai kings."

Most experts would argue that a level-wind reel with a quality drag and the capacity to hold at least 250 yards of 20- to 30-pound line is the choice. But Anderson caught the record his way. Like many river regulars, Anderson used Spin-N-Glos, a strange-looking cork body lure with rubber wings often used with a plastic, hootchie skirt and a big single hook. Add a few beads and the extremely ugly result is ready to go. The important thing is the proper selection from the hundreds of combinations in Spin-N-Glo and hootchie colors and sizes—locally called Kenai specials. There is one basic truth to these permutations. Whatever the hot combination or size, you'll be missing a vital component even if you tote 50 pounds of parts in a confusion of sizes and a rainbow of colors.

"Most of the guides on the river backtroll plugs," Anderson said. "This keeps clients from snagging bottom quite as often. My brother-in-law and I use really big Kenai Specials. We think big kings see them better in the murky water. I know a bit more than some about the smaller holes, and can handle our Kenai specials a bit better. So we'd look for tough spots to fish that held undisturbed kings.

"We had a nice Monarch aluminum boat with a 25 horsepower motor that got my brother-in-law, Bud Lofstedt, and me to the action. Sometimes we'd go down to Big Eddy Hole. Other times we would fish up at Morgan's Hole. We have some spots without names, too. Big kings hang in the current around pool heads and, if you work the lure right, it'll move right along with a drifting boat to cover lots of river bottom and tempt good fish."

Anderson's 100 Pounds Of Action

"The day we took the big fish we got out early before I had to go to the car agency. It was about seven in the morning when I hooked the fish. It immediately jumped over my brother-in-law's line, then ran off nearly 200 yards. We had to

Henry Schellert of Renton, Washington, landed this 85-pound king salmon taken on the Kenai River in Alaska. His big catch occurred June 11, 1989.

Kings Of The Kenai

follow it. It ran. We followed. Fortunately, we had room to work the fish. Good thing it wasn't Memorial Day. You wouldn't believe the crowds here on Memorial Day!"

Even without other boats to worry about, Anderson and Lofstedt nearly lost the fish. When Lofstedt tried to net the fish, he couldn't get enough of the fish's huge body into the net to lift it into the boat, and the big king flopped back in the river. So, after another couple of runs, they beached their boat on an island spit well downstream from the spot where Anderson first hooked the fish.

"I pulled and Bud pushed and we got the fish out on the sand," Anderson said. "It was so heavy we could barely drag it into our boat. We should have weighed it right away, but we stayed out. The Fish and Game biologist that weighed the fish said it probably lost 5 pounds. That would put it over 100 pounds."

Anderson's fish set a new IGFA 30-pound line class and both IGFA and NFWFHF all-tackle world records. It's now mounted and hangs in the Soldatna Peninsula Community Center.

Perspectives

This record seems certain to be broken. Alaska Fish and Game has a 104-pound king mounted on their headquarters wall that somebody netted. Several other salmon over 100 pounds have been netted or trolled up by commercial fishermen, too. The all-time monster came from a fish trap at Point Colpoys, Prince of Wales Island, Alaska in 1949. This fish weighed 126 pounds and measured 53½ inches in length and 38½ inches in girth, with a tail spread of 17½ inches.

Rod-and-reel line class records reflect this. Bob Carter took an 85½-pound salmon out of Hakai Pass. Howard C. Rider's 30-pound line class NFWFHF record weighed 93 pounds, and Heinz Wichman's unlimited line class record hit 92 pounds. The NFWFHF 45- and 50-pound line classes are open.

Several of the Chinook Salmon fly rod records seem within reach, too. Rick Sanchez set NFWFHF records in 2-, 4-, 6-, 8-, 10-, 12-, 14-, 16-pound line classes and unlimited chinook fly fishing records on Alaska's Talkeetna Mountain River between June 30, 1989 and July 4, 1989. The IGFA records for 2- and

4-pound tippets, both under 30 pounds, seem within reach. This might be the case in clear-water streams that are not clouded by silt.

Your best shot at record fish on conventional tackle might be the second-run fish on the Kenai River. Also, in Christopher Batin's excellent book, *How To Catch Alaska's Trophy Sportfish*, he suggests fishing in the Deep Creek-Anchor Point fishery on the east shore of Cook Inlet if you don't mind crowds at peak season. "Deep Creek has been called Alaska's fifth largest city on Memorial Day Weekend," Batin said. "And for good reason. Hundreds of resident and non-resident anglers come here to catch big kings. The late-June, early July run is made up of second run of 40- to 90-pound Kenai kings."

Kenai kings, particularly the "second-run" fish, may offer something else special besides size. To start, they spawn in the main river that, unlike the clear, tributary streams favored by the first-run fish, stays high all summer and into early fall. Alaskan biologists say, "Some Kenai kings apparently do not spawn and die on their return to their natal streams. Instead, they turn around and go back to sea." Locals call these fish "leatherbacks" because their skin texture looks like brown leather. These kings of the Kenai might not fit the sleek, silver salmon image, but one will, someday, pull the scales down past the magic century mark for some lucky fisherman.

Man-Made Salmon Magic

"Lower 48" salmon buffs may soon set records closer to home, too. Lake Michigan should support even larger salmon than Alaska, if the work of two Michigan State professors, Dr. Don Garling and Dr. Howard Tanner, develops as planned. With the cooperation of Michigan's Department of Natural Resources, and the usual underpaid school of graduate students, they developed a system to heat-shock salmon eggs.

This produces "triploidy" in nine of 10 salmon fry from the half of the eggs that survive. Why is this important? Triploid salmon are sterile. So they won't reproduce and overrun native species. Also, and more important for record seekers and those who like to eat their catch, instead of running up rivers and turning mushy before they spawn and die, they should remain bright and firm. They just chase bait in the Great Lakes and grow until caught by a happy fisherman.

The first of these fish were stocked in Lake Michigan and Lake Huron in 1986. Only about one percent of the total number of salmon stocked got the heat treatment. This was done so larger numbers of the expected big fish wouldn't decimate the forage and, if they got really huge, everything else in the Great Lakes.

How big will these fish grow? This depends on water quality, food availability and other factors. According to an informative article on the subject in the 1990 edition of the *IGFA World Record Game Fishes*, "If their experimental triploid salmon live long enough … this would mean new world records for the species." One can but hope!

14

Atlantic Salmon

Ken Jamieson had a very funny expression as he watched guide Charlie Adams release the biggest salmon seen on the Restigouche River in years. Jamieson, a Houston resident and long-time member of the Ristigouche Club, said, "It was the biggest fish I'd ever seen. Although, understandably, in the thrill of the moment I pictured it as a trophy fish, I was happy to serve the conservation cause and release the magnificent animal." Watching a 68½-inch-long fish with a 29-inch girth fin away, reflects today's attitude toward these wonderful fish. Atlantic salmon are too fine, too important and too beautiful to lose to sport or commercial overharvest.

Jamieson took his fish on a No. 4 Silver Rat fly fished off a 9-weight Orvis Boron, Graphite rod, a high tech reel and a 15-pound tippet. The big fish hit in the early evening. Jamieson was able to keep it in the river's main pool by the clubhouse during the hour and 15 minutes it took to bring it into tailing range of guide Charlie Adams. Given the heavy tippet and stout fly rod, it's easy to see why Atlantic salmon are so respected. For they fight hard, but fair, away from the hazards some fish seek.

Of course, Jamieson didn't have a real choice. Regulations prohibit keeping large Atlantic Salmon anywhere in the Western Hemisphere. So nobody knows exactly what Jamieson's fish weighed. The common girth and width formula would rate the fish at a fraction over 72 pounds. Lee Straight, director and past president of the Steelhead Society of British Columbia, thinks that Jamieson's fish weighed even more. (Atlantic salmon are very close to steelhead in their conformation.) He recommends instead, "the tried and true British Sturdy Formula which is four-thirds (1.3333333) times the length of the fish times the square of its girth, all divided by 1,000." Using this formula, Jamieson's catch would weigh 76.8 pounds. This is the largest Atlantic salmon taken on a fly.

European Records

Jamieson's released monster ranks just behind Hennrik Henricksen's 79-pound, 2-ounce fish taken on the Tana River in Norway in 1928. Henricksen took fish on a prawn or spoon by trolling—it seems unclear. Fly rod record salmon run nearly as large because, over most of its range and much of its history, salmon have been a fly rod fish caught by wealthy fishermen able to pay for an increasingly expensive sport.

In July 1921, Nicholas Denissoff, took a 56- and 74-pound fish on the same morning—some morning! The larger fish was the biggest ever taken on a fly rod. Charles Ritz, the world-famous hotelier and fly caster, said, "Denissoff was quite reliable as well as one of the few Russians smart enough to leave the country before the Bolsheviks with rather a large fortune."

An even bigger fish, a 103-pound, 2-ounce salmon, was reportedly "captured," probably with a net by poachers either in the river Devon or Forth in Scotland—accounts vary. Several other large Atlantic salmon were caught in Europe. One of the most famous British records was the 64-pound fish caught by Miss G. W. Ballantine on a spinning dace minnow bait in 1922. She fought it from the boat pool on the river Tay a half-mile downstream and landed it after a fight that went nearly two hours. All of these fish reflect the fact that bigger rivers, like those in Scandinavia, tend to produce larger size fish better able to fight strong flows.

In Europe, these salmon rivers have always been a tightly-held monopoly by landowners and the very rich who lease fishing rights. Good beats in Europe can run $3,000 a week or more per fisherman. So, Europeans have taken wonderful care of their fishery, and some of the largest Atlantic

This 60-pound Atlantic salmon is an example of the size of salmon in the Scandinavian countries. It was taken by Odd Haraldsen in 1965 from the Vosso River in Norway.

Atlantic Salmon

salmon ever ascend streams in Iceland, the British Isles, Norway and other Scandinavian countries. European salmon historically made their spawning runs into rivers from the Arctic Circle throughout the Baltic all the way down to Portugal. Since the French and Germans have trashed their rivers, their salmon are rare.

So, all the IGFA line class records, except 2- and 4-pound test, come from Europe.

Western Hemisphere Atlantic Salmon

"Keep" records are moot in the Western Hemisphere today. Neither states nor provinces allow fishermen to keep large salmon; most require flies only. So the big fish that are kept are from Iceland, Norway, Scotland and other European countries. The biggest mounted fish from the Western Hemisphere is the 55-pound Atlantic Salmon caught with a Lady Amherst fly by Esmond B. Martin on the Grand Cascapedia on June 27, 1939. It's displayed in the American Museum of Natural History and stretches 49¾ inches long and 30⅛ inches in girth.

In the United States, salmon fishing is more democratic, if now mostly catch and release, by specialists who love salar. Ever so slowly the fishery extends back to its historic range north from Long Island. Most of the New England rivers lost their salmon run when dams barred salmon runs during the industrial revolution, and logging removed shading trees so water temperatures rose so high that eggs could not hatch.

Today, the New England branch of the Atlantic Salmon Federation has moved local, state and federation agencies to provide fish ladders and such on these waters. Dams are starting to come down. Water quality gradually improves. Runs now extend in some waters as far south as the Connecticut River. Much more help is needed.

In Canada, salmon fishing runs from Ungava Bay in Northern Quebec down through the Maritime Provinces where salmon rivers, with wonderful names like the Restigouche, Matapedia or Grand Cascapedia, have long been regulated by lease and governmental decree. Fees on private water aren't low. Four rods might pay $4,000 to $4,800 for three days on the water with a lodge stay and guides. There is "open water" in most parts of Canada where fishing is available for a small fee.

Guide Charlie Adams is shown releasing a 72-pound Atlantic salmon taken in 1990 from the Restigouche River by Ken Jamieson.

In 1984, when salmon stocks reached a historic low, Canada announced a plan to " ... reestablish the vitality of a magnificent and important species." This plan included restrictions on commercial license allocations, gear restrictions (fly fishing only, for example), season reductions, by-catch limitations (these set seasonal limits), and license buy-back programs for the commercial limits. There were river closures and some closures of Newfoundland's Zone 12 and Maritime Province commercial fisheries.

Salar's Future

Fish like Jamieson's show that existing treaty provisions on the off-shore catch of Atlantic salmon, and strict freshwater restrictions have started the fishery on its way to recovery. More

Atlantic Salmon

work was needed. To see why this is an international problem, it's useful to see the Atlantic salmon life cycle. This starts with breeders running up into streams. Where dams are a problem, fish ladders or elevators are essential. So are adequate gravel spawning beds and decent water quality. Since females produce about 800 eggs per pound of body weight, regulations to protect large fish that are usually females are essential.

As the salar eggs hatch, the fry or "alevins" need adequate river flows and temperatures (stagnant or warm water reduces survival rate). At this point, the fry develop markings much like trout and become parr. This is a reason why trout fishing must be curtailed or "single barbless hooks, catch and release" on salmon rivers. Parr live in freshwater for two to six years. Then, they migrate downstream when they are about 5 to 7 inches long. As tidewater nears, parr lose their markings and become bright silver smolts.

In the ocean, smolts start to grow fast in the nutrient-rich waters off Nova Scotia and Prince Edward Island where they winter during their first year in the ocean. Then, as ocean waters cool, salmon run back into their wintering areas off the Grand Bank. With warming waters, salmon head north along the Hamilton, Nain and Sglek Banks of Labrador or swim toward western Greenland, before returning to their wintering grounds. On their third summer, they head unerringly back toward natal streams. European species follow a somewhat similar pattern.

The ½-pound to 7-pound "grilse" are exceptions to this pattern. They return to natal streams after their first year. Only grilse are kept in the Western Hemisphere by sportfishermen. Some grilse, like some main third summer returnees, survive spawning and go back to sea to return another year. Such fish are never as large as the huge fish that may live in the ocean for three, four or even five years before spawning.

The reason for the variation in time at sea for Atlantic salmon, and other sea-run fish like chinook salmon or steelhead, is simple. By staggering the number of years fish stay at sea before they return, nature "restocks" rivers on years when natural disasters like drought or even a Mount Saint Helens volcanic eruption might wipe out an age class.

Because of the international migrations of salmon, the

This mount of the 55-pound Atlantic salmon caught by Esmond Bradley Martin on Canada's Grand Caseapedia River in 1939 now hangs in the American Museum of Natural History.

North Atlantic Salmon Conservation Organization was formed in 1983 to set quotas to maintain stocks. In large part, this has resulted in lower commercial quotas off Newfoundland and Greenland and a prohibition of fishing outside the 200-mile limit. Unfortunately, there have been some "salmon pirates" in action around Iceland and in other areas. When advised of the problem on ships flying their flag, both the Poles and Danes stopped this illegal fishing. Panama should be next.

One way around this problem is to cease commercial fishing. Orri Vigfusson, an Icelander, is now trying to buy out the commercial fisheries in Greenland and the Faroe Islands. This would mean an additional 500,000 Atlantic salmon—half for North American waters, half for Europe—would reach their natal rivers.

Canada has also done a lot of rethinking about commercial fishing. It became obvious that the recreational use of salmon brings more money into Maritime Provinces than the commercial catch. For example, a recent study showed that, in 1988 commercial landings of Atlantic Salmon were valued at less than $4 million (Canadian) and the value of the recreational fishing in Newfoundland was about $20 million. Of the recreational fishing development in British Columbia, Ontario and New Brunswick, the study concludes "a high level of economic development based on recreational fishing activity can be built and sustained by a properly managed fish resource." Another study showed that a commercially caught salmon was valued at less than $20 in 1988, but an angled salmon's value exceeds $170 each.

The problem, as with other species, is that commercial fishermen do not want to lose their traditional lifestyles, even if they are paid not to fish. This problem seems difficult to overcome. It is gradually falling into place as, with reduced stocks of salmon, the fishery becomes marginally cost effective for commercial fishermen.

However, readers should know that organizations like the Atlantic Salmon Foundation do a lot more than give banquets and contribute money. They can pressure politicians. They can insist that existing laws about water quality and river flows are enforced. Perhaps most important, by their efforts, they let everyone know that fishermen are watching.

=15=

Lake Trout—
Laggard Lunkers

ake trout dredged up out of deep water on wire or lead-core line don't test anglers. Many find them a bit oily to eat, too. So, it's nice that most fish from Great Bear Lake, the site of all the IGFA lake trout records except the three of Ray Johnson's line class taken at Flaming Gorge, are carefully released. Larry Daunis, a resident of the Detroit area who set dozens of line class records during a contest, kept his, the 65-pound world record trolled up with 15-pound-test line from the Smith Arm of Great Bear in 1970 with a Three of Diamonds spoon. It proved impossible to contact Daunis, but Marlin Coulombe's 46-pound fish taken on 8-pound-test line offers the same scenario and a superior line test to fish-weight ratio.

Cruising To A Record With Coulombe

Coulombe, a U.S. Postal Service employee from Sacremento, California, part-time outdoor writer and a booking representative for several Great Bear Lake lodges, said, "I was fishing with my buddy, Trevor Slaymaker, who holds the NFWFHF 2-pound line class record for lakers with a 38-pound fish he caught in 1987. We were fishing in 10 to 20 feet of water near the lodge. We trolled with custom rods and large spoons, either Lucky Strike's or Len Thompson's.

"It was a really beautiful day. It started out foggy, but cleared up so we could see 40 feet or so down into the water.

We'd been out on the Smith Arm of the lake since the morning. It's light almost 24 hours a day that time of year, so you really get a day's fishing if you don't sleep much.

"We had already taken a 43-pound fish on 80-pound test. That would have been a world record in that seldom-used line class, but the line tested too light. So the fish got bounced down a class, and didn't qualify. We lost two other fish that would have given Trevor the IGFA line class record when my 46-pound record fish hit in the early afternoon. Trevor also managed to lose a fish at the net that we figured weighed about 40 pounds. After I caught my fish, he lost another, about 30 pounds, on 2-pound test line. You might say we had a really great day on the water. At least if you don't count lost fish! I know we didn't want to come in."

Record Details

Coulombe trolled 6-pound test Berkley Trilene on a 10½-foot Berkley Noodle Rod and a Lucky Strike Wave lure.

"It took about 40 minutes to get the fish in the net," Coulombe said. "Trevor got him first dip. So we headed for shore and weighed the fish while it was still alive. We try to do that with fish close to the record. You don't want to waste any fish. Besides, the little ones taste better.

"We are expecting to top the 2-, 4- and 80-pound test line classes this summer and bring all the lake trout line class records back to Great Bear Lake. Most of them will be set from Trophy Lodge on the Smith Arm. I hope to get a shot at the arctic char record, too, if we make it to Tree River as planned."

Given Coulombe's matter-of-fact attitude, it's useful to remember that lake trout do not come easily except in Northwest Territory waters like the Great Bear Lake. Even there fishermen need adequate tackle and a clear understanding with their guide that they are out for records instead of merely lots of fish.

Looking At Lakers

While lake trout are definitely the biggest trout in North America, most are neither a bagful of fight if taken with usual deep-water methods nor fast growing. As a result, lakers are a quality quarry only on light tackle where you can catch them

The NFWFHF's 8-pound class record lake trout is this 46-pound fish taken by Marlin Coulombe from Great Bear Lake in Canada's Northwest Territories. It measured 51 inches in length.

Lake Trout—Laggard Lunkers

within 20 feet of the surface. However, because of the slow growth, it can take 25 years for a Great Bear Lake laker to reach 25 inches. Lakers don't stand up to fishing pressure well. So fishermen able to afford the $2,900-a-week tariff at Great Bear Lake lodges during the short seven-week season have a lock on this kind of action.

Only in the huge Northwest Territory lakes, like Great Bear, can fishermen see lakers swimming 40 feet deep. Only in such waters do you consistently find lunker lakers. This is definitely fly-in fishing and limited in season. Large ice floes can prohibit boat travel on the lake as late as July, and the season closes around Labor Day.

"Our guides depend on temperature to find fish," Coulombe said. "The main lake won't warm up as much, or as fast, as the shallow bays that hold more food. So we start fishing at about 10 feet where we find rocky shorelines. We do keep an eye out for whitefish jumping to escape lurking lakers."

It's worth noting that big lakers are often a bit lazy and tend to hit slower-worked spoons—at least one study shows bigger fish in a species may prefer slightly colder water than the species optimum. According to most experts, you don't need any sort of heavy wire leader. A short shock tippet can be handy when playing lakers for long periods, or when fish sound around rocks. See IGFA regulations.

Coulombe also said, "While you can fish nearly 24 hours a day, the best fishing is found nearer shore when the light is a bit low—say, before 8 a.m. and from 7 p.m. to midnight. However, most of the fishermen just move out to deeper water during the rest of the day. When you only have a week, you don't rest much."

Down And Dirty Lower 48 Lakers

Lake trout dredged up from 300-foot depths of Lake Tahoe, even the 20-plus pound fish now rarely taken, don't offer much fight on wire or lead-core line. That's standard for the "lower 48" states where the average laker runs smaller and deeper than would be the case in Canada.

Great Lakes fishermen, Lake Tahoe specialists and other anglers have started to move away from wire line. Many experts now use monofilament off downriggers with releases in areas

Lake Tahoe yielded this pair of lake trout, the larger of which weighed 20 pounds, 6 ounces. It was good for first place in an annual contest conducted at the lake. The angler? The author of this book.

with reasonably even bottom that minimize hang-ups. On calm days or days with mild winds, deep-water jigging can produce with large drails, a sort of hyperthyroid jig, some of which weigh up to a pound. This only works where boats can remain stationary over 100 to 150 feet of water.

A few spots in the Great Lakes offer river-mouth action. Most of these streams offer easy catches where it is legal to fish. Lake trout in rivers act like browns, and natives rarely grow large, probably because they are so easy to catch.

Perspectives

Northwest Territories Tourism has at least one mounted laker that would top 100 pounds. So bigger fish than Larry Daunis' 65-pound, all-tackle world record set in 1970 seem a certainty. Ray Johnson's 40- and 50-pound and unlimited line class records set on Flaming Gorge Reservoir in 1984 and 1985 seem threatened.

Fly fishing records are downright silly. Lawrence E. Hudall set five records in 1986. The cane pole record is, not surprisingly, open. The image of a fisherman on one end of a 20-foot cane pole with a 20- or 30-pound laker on the other end does boggle the mind—it might tempt the reckless. This might be "interesting" as a variation on the old Japanese barbless lure system used by commercial tuna boats in years past. Although a green laker in a 16-foot boat might wreck tackle havoc!

The open 14- and 16-pound fly rod tippet classes might suit purists. Given the proper conditions, catching a laker chasing whitefish on the surface with a "dry fly" like a huge Muddler Minnow would seem relatively simple. Otherwise, sinking lines and cigar-size flies might be needed.

Fly rod IGFA records, as is often the case, are a bit more realistic, but hardly out of reach. The IGFA line test records, such as Salt Lake City resident Ray Johnson's 2-, 4- and 80-pound test records—all around 30 pounds—are quite substantial, too. It looks like record seekers need to go to Great Bear Lake with fly or noodle rods. With the right site and close attention to IGFA regulations on double lines and leaders, at least five records seem within easy reach.

=16=

Rainbow Trout—Fathers And Sons

The casual observer, or today's interviewer, might think that David White used up a lifetime's luck on his 42-pound, 2-ounce all-tackle world record rainbow trout. He was eight years old in 1970, and motor mooching with herring for salmon off Bell Island, Alaska, with his father, Robert White, a Seattle-area dentist.

"We fished out of an inflatable with floorboards and used 25-pound-test line on our usual gear and rigged herring," David said. "I don't really remember anything special. It took about 35 to 40 minutes to land the fish. He was still fighting when we netted him. He was blind in one eye. So when he swam by the boat he couldn't see the net. We got him weighed, frozen and sent him to Seattle. The taxidermy outfit started to process the fish, but the guy thought the fish looked funny.

"Fish and Game sent experts down and they took scale samples and a whole bunch of measurements. The newspaper came out and took my photo. It seemed like a lot of fuss at the time."

The "fuss" should seem to be no surprise. According to Chris Batin, the IGFA representative in Alaska and author of two authoritative Alaskan fishing guides, "White's fish is probably a 'one of.'" Most of the other big steelhead we see are in the 30-pound range at best." Had the story stopped here it would seem rather matter-of-fact, more a question of luck than skill, and not particularly interesting.

Still there are questions. If the record was weighed on a certified scale, why didn't someone notice the fish was a salmon? Especially since the person that weighed the fish was a fish and game expert! To the even modestly expert the fish are quite identifiable.

Then, too, a fish that size sounds like a load for an 8-year-old. Did David really reel in his catch, or did his father help, as fathers have been known to do? On the other hand, if cheating went on, how come the species was accidentally discovered only after the fish was mounted?

Interviews with David's father and others in the area turned up the full, and much more interesting story. David's father still has, as might be expected, vivid memories of that day. Dr. White, whose dental practice extends into Alaska, wasn't your typical tourist fisherman, either. David White was far more than a first-time beginner, too.

Dr. White spends part of each month in Seattle, and the rest of his working time in often remote Alaskan towns and villages that do not have a dentist. Patients wait for his regular rounds. So Dr. White is able to enjoy both urban and bush lifestyles. He shares these lifestyles with his wife, daughter and three sons.

As Dr. White said, "A lot of people thought we were crazy. We often fished together out of our Avon. After jamming the family and our gear into a Beaver we would fly into remote lakes and spend time together. We used to stay in tents, fix our own food and catch our own fish. The day we got the record we had the whole family aboard."

Dr. White and his family flew into Bell Island on an afternoon float plane charter out of Ketchikan, flopped their 16-foot Avon sport boat on the floating dock at the Bell Island Resort and pumped it up. Everyone helped load the boat, and they set off powered by a 10 horsepower Johnson. Their 16-foot Avon, the old model with wooden floorboards and transom, was jammed.

Dr. White ran the motor from the stern. His wife and daughter huddled in the bow out of the spray. Dr. White's little girl was too young to fish. So she sat in the bow and shared stories with her mother. The three boys, swaddled in wet weather gear, were shoe-horned into the center seat with, as

A young David R. White (in 1970) is shown with the 42-pound, 2-ounce IGFA and NFWFHF rainbow trout all tackle record holder taken in a stiff battle off Bell Island, Alaska.

Dr. White remembers it, "the bare minimum of pushing, shoving and elbowing after being cooped up in the chartered Beaver."

Dr. White didn't need a guide. They had the right tackle, knew the area well and had fished for years. Gear wasn't really special. Each boy faced aft. Each held a medium-weight rod with a Penn-revolving spool reel filled with 40-pound-test line tied to a 30-pound leader. These rigs suited mooching with rigged herring in the Glory Hole just across the channel from the resort.

Six in a small inflatable in Alaskan waters might sound dangerous. It wasn't; these waters were reasonably sheltered. Everyone wore life jackets, and there were many other boats about. The daily Bell Island fishing tournament drew big crowds! Other boaters later insured IGFA certification of David White's record by testifying that "only the boy played the fish."

The White boys had rods out to port and starboard, and a third line out over the transom that, at least some of the time, cleared Dr. White's head. The boys had noted some big salmon at the weigh-in station, so they paid very close attention to their tackle.

Dr. White followed the standard procedure for salmon

trollers in the area. He idled the motor and drifted "The Wall" and "Glory Hole" as the boys' big mooched herring baits turned slowly just off bottom. Then, he kicked the outboard into forward, and slowly motor-mooched out off the point before drifting back.

A huge reversal current with slack water in the center makes this spot ideal for record attempts at certain tide stages. Once a fish was hooked, boaters could easily move over into slack water and play the fish there, or, if both smart and skilled, maneuver their boats so the fish had to fight the current as well as the angler.

About 8:30 in the evening while they trolled past the point, David got what Dr. White calls, "the big hit." Dr. White followed the fish as he and his wife got other kids to reel in. David's fish ran several hundred yards, fortunately toward slack water. Once out of the way of other fishermen, Dr. White shut down the motor, and the big, black Avon drifted in the current.

David had braced his feet against the floorboards and watched line peel off his reel. He could do little against the strong pull of the fish. After the first run slowed, he started to pump. He pumped hard and gained line. Much of the line lost on the first run built, sweaty inch by sweaty inch, back on the reel. Then, slowly, with that unstoppable slow, steady pull typical of big salmon, line again peeled off David's reel. He pumped, pulled and struggled until it was too much for an 8-year-old to handle.

"Dad," he said, "You've got to help."

Dr. White replied, "Okay, but you got a big fish. If we take the rod, you can never say you caught the fish."

"Dad, I'm really tired."

"Son, you can let drag off and work one arm at a time. Or you can let your brothers play the fish."

With his brothers yelling about helping, and "their fish," there was no way David would let them touch his rod. He had a lot of spunk, and had fished since he was four. So he would crank down on the drag and fight the fish; then, loosen the drag and rest when he got tired until he could fight again. "It started to get dark," Dr. White said, "but the fish seemed a bit closer. David was exhausted. The big fish kept circling. The circles drew nearer and nearer. So, I got my big net ready and moved everyone on the other side of the boat. You've got to worry about line hanging up in an inflatable, and I needed a place to dump the fish. If I got it!

"I couldn't figure out why, as the fish kept circling, it came in closer and closer. David could no longer put on that much pressure. Then, the fish came right down the side of the boat. I scooped. It was just like a waterfall. The huge fish flopped in the boat as I held it down with the net. Later, we found out the fish didn't avoid the boat because it was blind on that side.

"At this point pandemonium broke out. We thought David had caught a great big king salmon. The other boys screamed to make more trolling runs. David seemed stunned, but not ready to quit. So we fished until dark. Then, went back in to the resort with the kids screaming and yelling about the big fish. So when we got to the dock, people were hanging around and weighing fish. A couple of fishermen, who had weighed big fish, waited to see ours. Everyone who watched the long fight wanted to see what the 'little kid in the funny boat' had caught."

Dr. White was extremely lucky that summer. An Alaskan fish and wildlife officer at dockside took scale samples and such. By now, it was dark. The kids leaped around and made wild guesses about the fish's weight. When the scales finally settled, the officer recorded David's fish as the biggest salmon of the day. He had won the daily contest.

Dr. White planned to steak and eat the big fish because it was too large for their coolers. Fortunately, the fish and game official and the resort owner, an old friend, told Dr. White that, "Your son may never catch another salmon as big as this. You really should have it mounted." Dr. White wasn't convinced, but David really wanted the fish mounted.

So when the fish and game official offered to handle the freezing, and Dr. White found out they could recover the meat from the taxidermist in Seattle, he agreed. Walt Shaw, an old buddy of Dr. White's dumped the fish into a freezer. Dr. White and his family stayed in tents, so they had no real way to handle the fish that was far too big for their coolers in any case. When they got the fish back the next morning, it was boxed for transport. So nobody every really saw the fish in daylight, and they flew back to Seattle.

Sometime later Dr. White went to the taxidermist to recover David's salmon.

"The fellow kept asking all these questions," he said. "I started to get really annoyed. I couldn't understand it. It sounded like he was accusing David and me of cheating on the catch. That made me a bit angry, but even more curious. I wondered why he wanted all the details, and why he was so interested. So I told him that David had no help, and gave him the other information he requested."

Finally, after shaking his head, the taxidermist said, "Unless I don't know fish, and I've mounted hundreds, this isn't a salmon. This is a steelhead, and a world record. However, once in a while Atlantic salmon, reared for sale in pens down in the sound escape. It's barely possible this could be one of these. Give me some scale samples, and we'll let Dr. Donaldson at the University certify the fish. That way, if it's the record, you'll meet IGFA requirements."

After Dr. Donaldson certified the fish as a steelhead, or sea-run rainbow trout, Dr. White's life got complicated. First, they had to give the IGFA a line sample. Fortunately, each boy had his own rod. Then Dr. White had to fly an IGFA representative out to Bell Island to check the resort scales and locate witnesses to the weighing and catch. Fortunately, the scale was still there and witnesses supported David's claim. So, IGFA now knew what the weight reading was, and the modification they needed to make to get a true weight.

Finally, IGFA needed a certified statement from the fish and wildlife official who weighed the fish. It took time to locate him, he had been moved to northern Alaska. The officer still remembered David, the big fish and the night weigh-in. So, he wrote up the needed documentation. IGFA understandably, considering the importance of the record and the rather odd circumstances, took six months to certify the record. It may stand for some time. Only one larger sea-run rainbow trout—commonly known as "steelhead"—is known, and it was taken in a net.

17

Brown Trout— Bags Of Big Browns

Michael Manley should have used a single hook the night he headed out with two friends to McClellan's Trout Dock on Arkansas' North Fork River, a tailwater river which is only about four or five miles in length. If he had, he would own the IGFA all-tackle world record for brown trout as well as his NFWFHF all-tackle and 8-pound test records. For, under IGFA regulations, fishermen are limited to a couple of single hooks with bait in order to prevent snagging and other abuses; trebles are only allowed on plugs. So when Tony Solomon took his NFWFHF record 30-pound, 8-ounce brown on a Rebel plug (trebles are legal on plugs), he qualified for the IGFA 5-to-1 club.

Fourteen-year-old David Jones Wooten doubled with a 34-pound brown for the NFWFHF record on 17-pound line and the IGFA 16-pound line class record. Carl Jones took a "10-to-1 Club" 20-pound, 12-ounce IGFA record brown on 2-pound test on the Arkansas' White River. Stanford Shanker's 27-pound, 9-ounce IGFA 4-pound-line record hit on the White River. Clearly, something wonderful happened to brown trout in the 1980s on the adjacent White and North Fork Rivers.

Even though the current IGFA all-tackle brown, a 35-pound, 15-ounce fish, was taken by Eugenio Cavalia out of Nahuel Huapi in Argentina in 1952, and you hear rumors of massive European brown trout, there's no question that the North Fork and White Rivers in Arkansas offer your best possible chance at a world record.

Manley's Monster

Michael Manley wouldn't argue about this. Interest in the White and North Fork Rivers peaked when "Manley's Monster" smashed state and world records. While his 38-pound, 9-ounce brown may qualify as a happy accident, Manley certainly displayed professional fish-playing skills, and, as is always the case with records, enjoyed considerable luck after the fish ate his bait.

Manley and his buddies, Paul Suddeth and Tom Long, got a late start. They didn't even arrive at McClellan's Trout Dock until after 11 p.m. on a Saturday when they had really planned to go frogging. Since you could "steam cook" in Arkansas' summer even after dark, they headed for the dock and the cool waters of the White River, the outlet of Bull Shoals Lake.

Manley's gear, a light 5-foot spinning outfit, better suited panfish than monster browns. He rigged a small treble hook on a dropper and baited with corn and marshmallows, a local favorite bait for recently stocked trout. Corn attracts trout and the marshmallow floats the bait a dropper's length off bottom. Manley cast, but lost his bait to small trout. He cast again with the same result. Anxious not to be cleaned again, he set his hook at the first gentle tap on his third cast.

Six times Manley worked the fish up to the dock. Six times it spooked as Manley's "helpers" tried to net the fish. On the "lucky seventh" attempt, Long got the brown into the net. The net's bow bent at right angles under the weight of Manley's monster brown. Manley jumped into the shallows, grabbed the net's bow and handle and hauled his prize onto the dock.

Then, with the state record in mind, the three "happy hookers" woke a guide. "Manley's Monster" pulled the scale down 5 pounds past the state record. More calls awakened sleepy experts. Mark Oliver, a district fisheries biologist joined the gawking group at the local all-night convenience store. They saw the largest brown ever taken on a rod and reel in North America.

Backup Browns

Many other large browns have hit lures and gobbled bait on

A smiling Mike Manley holds the 38-pound, 9-ounce IGFA and NFWFHF record brown trout that he reeled in from the North Fork River in northern Arkansas in 1988.

the White River in its 120-mile run of prime brown trout water below Bull Shoals Lake. This action started back in the 1940s when a few fingerling browns were dumped into the North Fork River which feeds into the White. It seems quite appropriate that brown trout native to Europe, which were first stocked in the United States by Baron Lucius von Behr (hence "German browns") now reach their largest sizes in waters to which they are not native.

Loch Leven trout, as you might guess from the name, are the stillwater strain of brown trout from Scotland. These fish apparently do not reach quite the sizes of German browns. Both types have cross-bred to the point that they are now considered one species.

Once these first small stockings from the White River

reproduced in the wild, fishing clubs improved spawning conditions with Vibert boxes, small containers buried in stream gravels that improve egg and fry survival. The river trout action took off. Water drawn from deep, below-reservoir surfaces insure temperatures perfect for growth all year. Small browns get a "jump start" with incredible amounts of freshwater shrimp. Once fish reach about 18 inches, they switch to the two types of sculpins and the plentiful crayfish on the rivers. Then, when the shad in the reservoirs die off from temperature drops in the winter, shad fragments ground by turbine blades and whole shad are everywhere. When very large fish need only open their mouth to grab dead shad, they can put on a pound or more in a few weeks. As a bonus, not that one is needed, Fish and Game stocks lots of put-and-take rainbows. These catchables, along with the native chubs and suckers, are just right for big-brown dinners. At least one expert estimates that approximately "over 30 percent of the trout we stock end up in big brown trout."

So a monster Rebel painted in rainbow trout color is a hot lure. To top it off, Fish and Game has a hatchery on the five-mile-long North Fork River that dumps a ton of trout food into its ponds daily. Some of this washes into the river, too! So browns get big fast. How fast? A 6-inch planter ballooned up into a 10-pound brown in three years!

Given this you would expect the rivers to be overrun with fishermen. They certainly crowd up during summer, and on holiday weekends. Still, over 100 miles of the White River offers plenty of places for big browns to hide. Depending on the water levels, some sections of the river are more of a challenge than some boaters can handle. However, the main reason browns can avoid fishermen is their nocturnal habits. They simply are not out and active when most anglers are on the water. As a result, most big browns are caught by specialists, or the simply lucky, who fish after dark.

Tony Solomon's Persistence Pays

Tony Solomon ranks as a specialist. His catch reflects much more preparation, planning and perseverance than Manley's. Solomon, who had fished the White River (mostly at night) for 29 years, faced a unique problem early in the morning on

The North Fork River in Arkansas also yielded this 30-pound, 8-ounce German brown which is the record for the NFWFHF's 6-pound line class. This fish was taken by Tony Solomon in 1986.

August 31, 1986. He looked into the live well at the 11-pound female brown he had caught about an hour earlier; then, looked at the hooked jaw male brown in his net.

"I could see they both wouldn't fit in there and there just wasn't any question in my mind what to do—I turned the 11-pounder lose," he said.

Solomon wasn't that upset about the release even though action on the river usually slows after Labor Day. After all, this St. Louis electrician drives down to spend 40 weekends a year on the North Fork and White Rivers. He specializes in light-tackle lure fishing and knows both rivers well. So he catches batches of big browns. Besides, at the time he had a pending IGFA 2-pound line class world record brown that had weighed in at 14 pounds, 6 ounces. Then, too, Solomon wanted to keep the male that thrashed in his net wet until it was weighed. So, he jammed the fish, net and all, into his livewell. The fish folded double. Now Solomon had to worry about getting the fish out of the livewell. He even considered cutting the net!

"I couldn't believe it," Solomon said, "I used to think if I could just break 20 pounds, I'd be content."

The fish that snapped up Solomon's 6-inch jointed Rebel at

about 2 a.m. ran a bit bigger than 20 pounds—10½ pounds bigger to be exact!

Solomon often fishes all night because the river is quiet and browns feed best after the sun is off the water. He used a standard jerk and twitch retrieve, and the fish hooked itself. Then, he carefully played the fish for 30 minutes before it came to the net. His fish demolished the old 6-pound-test record set in Flaming Gorge, Utah, in 1978. It was just one of 12 brown trout over 20 pounds in weight taken from the White River in a six-week period in July and August.

Local Options

According to fish and game experts, fishermen who cannot get to the White or North Fork may find their own hotspots for brown trout. One California expert said, "We have huge browns in most two-story reservoirs with bass and trout, but nobody fishes with a big enough lure or bait to interest these double-digit fish." A Colorado biologist said, "Tailwaters that stay between 45 and 60 degrees all year downstream from reservoirs almost always hold big browns and other trout." All suggested that night fishing be considered where legal!

18

Six Pounds Of Crappie Confusion

Fishermen catch black crappie in every state except Alaska and Hawaii. "Big" black crappie run a couple of pounds. Line class record fish, and the IGFA all-tackle record, barely top 4 pounds. Then, there is Lettie Robinson's colossal 6-pound monster! That is the Moby Dick of black crappie! But, like Captain Ahab, Lettie Robinson has disappeared. The best efforts of the State of Louisiana's Inland Fisheries Department can't find her. She most likely has moved, and probably changed her name when she married. After all, she was only 12 or 13 years old when she caught her colossal crappie on November 28, 1969.

Howard Rogillio, still at the Louisiana Inland Fisheries Department, remembers seeing and weighing that "long ago" fish. So does Denny Fantaneau, now chief of the department for the state of Louisiana. It was the first record fish he ever examined.

As he told the story recently, "I had just got out of school, and it's been a long, long time since I saw the fish. At the time, I didn't classify the fish as either a white or a black crappie. That turned out to be a big mistake. I can't remember why I didn't classify it right away. Guess I was too excited. Of course, Louisiana didn't, until recently, have separate records for white and black crappie.

"I sure remember the girl. She was only 12 or 13 and she got real excited over the fish. She seemed overwhelmed with the whole thing at the time." He continued, "I was called late, as I remember it, and went right on over. The fish was huge, at least two pounds bigger than I ever expected a crappie to get. I remember looking at the fish and laughing to myself about the fact that she caught it with a cheap cane pole with a worm in the seaplane canal."

The seaplane canal is a long, dredged landing area full of water that seaplanes still use for an airstrip. It's technically known as "Westwege Canal" although no local person calls it by that name.

Fantaneau said, "Lettie Robinson didn't have fancy tackle either. She had an old cane pole, battered and brown, that looked like it had lived a couple of hard years in a shed. There was a clump of cheap line wound on the pole with a wine cork float, and a small, and I think, rusty hook. She baited with some worms from the yard toted in a can. Landing that fish on that gear must have been a real circus.

"We didn't make much of the record at the time. I'm not sure if she even kept the fish. I seem to remember she did. Wouldn't it be wonderful if, somewhere, there was a 6-pound black crappie mounted on a wall?"

He continued, "She came back later with paperwork to file for the records. She also had a pretty good snapshot of the catch. I checked the photo carefully and, from the spine count, it was clear the fish was a record black crappie. I know it was a black crappie. I can't imagine why the IGFA doesn't recognize it as a record."

IGFA representative Mike Leech said, "That was back before we took over the records from *Field & Stream*. I guess the reason the fish wasn't allowed was the time lapsed between catch and record application, or the fact the fish wasn't identified by a fisheries biologist."

The cane pole she used couldn't have been the problem. The IGFA allowed T.S. Hudson's all-tackle bluegill taken on a cane pole, and Dr. C. C. Abbot's yellow perch—as discussed in Chapter 1—was most likely taken in the same way. It couldn't be the line test either; after all nobody knows what Dr. Abbot used. Perhaps, the refusal to grandfather-in this record reflects the fact that the IGFA concentrates more on saltwater and game species. Clearly the fish has been properly identified!

This 2-pound, 8-ounce crappie, caught by Elmer Barnes in 1965, once held the IGFA's world line class record for 8-pound test. The record in that line class now stands at 4 pounds, 8 ounces on a catch in 1981 by Carl Herring Jr.

Howard Rogillio, a fisheries biologist like his friend Fantaneau, backs up the Robinson claim.

Rogillio said, "Sure, I saw the fish. And I remember the photograph. I remember thinking it was a huge black crappie, and it was wonderful to see how excited the young lady got. She could barely stand still. I looked at the photograph, too. It was a good one and showed the fish to be a black crappie."

He continued, "You can't miss that identification based on fin rays and other factors. White crappie have dark markings that form bars and six spines on their dorsal fin; black crappie have irregular markings and seven to eight spines at the front of their dorsal fins. It's a shame only the NFWFHF lists the fish. She should have the IGFA all-tackle record, too. It's a wonderful record."

Six Pounds Of Crappie Confusion

The Other Records

Just how wonderful a 6-pound black crappie is only becomes apparent when considered in light of other IGFA and NFWFHF records. The IGFA line class records run from 3-pound, 2-ounce to 4-pound, 4-ounce fish. White crappie records, the only other possibility for the Robinson catch, are smaller. The IGFA all-tackle black crappie weighed 4 pounds, 8 ounces; the white crappie all-tackle records pulled the scale down to 5 pounds, 3 ounces.

NFWFHF recognizes the Robinson fish as the all-tackle black crappie record. This seems one of the rare cases where they are right and the IGFA is in error! Examination of these old records, and a "best evidence" rule would make sense. Perhaps we need a double set of standards, like Florida's, that lists "uncertified records" and "certified records."

The Real Question

If Dr. C. C. Abbot's 4-pound, 3-ounce yellow perch caught in May 1965 is allowed, why isn't Lettie Robinson's record, an equally outstanding catch that has been identified by two skilled fisheries biologists and properly weighed, allowed?

=19=

Super Shellcrackers

When one 202-acre pond gives up seven state and two world record fish in a row, you have a super spot, even if it is hardly a secret. Florida's Merritts Pond qualifies as just that for the chubby redear sunfish that local people affectionately call "shellcrackers." So 17-year-old Joey Floyd knew he had a shot at a record and, he hoped, a chance to skip school the March morning he took his super sunfish. He and his father, Marion, hit the pond at dawn on a damp, drizzly Florida day that suited fishing better than the Chamber of Commerce. All fishermen are optimists, but Joey Floyd had more reason than most to expect big fish. The last world record fish, C. L. Windham's 4-pound, 10-ounce monster, was caught here just the year before. So Joey isn't surprised that he hooked his "hooky fish" on a cricket.

As Floyd remembers it, "We were fishing holes in floating weeds that morning. I had already picked up about a half-dozen bream—bluegills to Yankees—and a nice shellcracker when the big one picked up a cricket I had pitched out on the bottom.

"I didn't see the fish hit, but from the pull I thought it was a bass because the fish tangled itself in the grass. It took seven or eight minutes to work him back to the boat. He kept diving for bottom. I couldn't see him. The grass is really thick in the pond. I'd pull him free and he'd dive back. Of course, my pa kept giving me all sorts of advice, but I was too busy to listen most of the time as I tried to pull the fish free.

"Then, I had trouble getting the fish into the landing net. In all, it took nearly 10 minutes to net the fish. The line broke just after we got the net and the fish into the boat."

Floyd said, "We didn't know how big the fish ran at first. I fished another hour until it was time to go to school. We ended up with about three dozen fish before Dad had to go to work. Then, when we weighed the fish on non-certified scales, it ran a couple of ounces over 5 pounds. I knew I had school beat that day, when we had to go and find the right kind of scale."

Floyd's fine fish finally weighed in at 4 pounds, 13¾ ounces, and its girth measured only an inch less than its 17½- inch length. After contacting Florida fish and game officials and meeting them at a certified scale, Joey and his father had the fish checked with a metal detector, weighed and identified by Norman Young, a regional fisheries biologist and photographed by Stan Kirkland. Both were Florida Game and Fresh Water Fish Commission officials. The final weight was later certified as the Florida, IGFA and NFWFHF all-tackle and line test records. Florida, it should be noted, offers two kinds of records. Older records or those not carefully checked, are "uncertified." "Certified" records are very, very carefully examined. So a Florida "certified record" should have little trouble being accepted by either major record-keeping body.

"I think the record helped put me on the right road," Floyd said. "I'd had a little trouble in school, but after the record I got things together. I've got a good job now with the State Department of Corrections, too.

"Everyone made a bit of a fuss over the fish and that changed things for me. I still haven't caught another large one. Now that I'm working, I've less time to fish, but I always go back in March and April."

Except for the $10,000 Trilene prize for a record fish offered by Berkley, the record doesn't seemed to have impressed Floyd that much. He said, "I caught it on a plain, old 63-inch-long Zebco Pro Staff rod and reel with 10-pound-test Trilene line and a 6-pound-test Bonnyl Leader with a No. 6 Mustad hook with a cricket for bait."

It's likely that Floyd's attitude relates to the age of the pond and the likelihood of another Merritts Pond record. The pond

This redear sunfish, or shellcracker as it's known in the South, tipped the scales at 4 pounds, 13¾ ounces. It was a record for Joey Floyd, Marianna, Florida, who caught the fish in nearby Merritts Mill Pond.

Super Shellcrackers

formed when settlers first dammed up Robinson's Big Spring Creek to power a gist mill ín the 1800s. The local people raised the dam and later expanded the pond for use as a low-head hydroelectric power source.

It's far from a typical shallow, tannin-colored Southern lake; its crystal waters wander three or four meandering miles up the old creek channel back through second-growth trees. So the lake itself is only 150 yards or so wide. These fertile waters support incredible concentrations of the aquatic snails that give "shellcrackers" their Southern name.

Stan Kirkland, the fisheries biologist who photographed Joey Floyd's record fish, said, "Fishing should improve in the lake. We drew the pond down in 1990 and took about 200 to 300 redear sunfish out of the lake to hold in tanks for spawning. When we did this, we picked up six or eight 3½- to 4-pound fish, all females, that probably died of post-spawn stress. This isn't unusual. When unseasonable rains refilled the pond, water clarity declined. This could mean new record fish in the next few years if development and other factors don't change the pond."

Experts expect that the increased algae count and the addition of new nutrients, as high-and-dry shoreline vegetation decays after the drawdown will broaden the base of the food chain. This is a major reason new reservoirs offer peak action just after they reach full-pool. At Merritts Pond, Kirkland reports 5,000 to 10,000 baby bluegills and shellcrackers milling about in a 12-foot-deep hole just off a dock.

In the next few years, Merritts Pond should produce sacks of 2½-pound and larger redear sunfish that qualify for the Florida "Big Catch" full-color citation. All you need to do is remember that Marianna, Florida, locals call the fish "shellcrackers" and the location "mill pond."

20

Bluegills a.k.a. Bream

Certainly as could be expected, A. J. McClane said it best. In the *Secret Life Of A Bream Specialist*, one of the quality columns George Reiger selected in his fine book *Fishing With McClane*, McClane said, "It would require supernatural aid to sing the praises of a fish whose rustic charm far exceeds his capacity for prolonged struggle. But, when caught on very light tackle, there is a patent of nobility about the bream."

Bluegills, a.k.a. "Bream," aren't bad in the pan either. As McClane continued, "A king might fare no better than on a feast of swamp cabbage, hushpuppies and deep-fried bream ... It may be that panfish are strikingly similar in dimensions, coloring and morality, but as the meek inherit the earth, so the bream has inherited the water. He is the most sought, caught, prolific fish in our land."

Given such a democratic fish, willing, even anxious to be caught by even the most undeserving, it's a shame that a mere 2 ounces of bream can make a man so unhappy for so long. In 1950, when T.S. Hudson broke Coke McKenzie's 1947 4-pound, 10-ounce world record with a 4-pound, 12-ounce fish from Mr. McKenzie's favorite fishing hole, McKenzie wasn't happy.

In the 40 years since, T.S. Hudson and his fish have long since disappeared. Little is known about Hudson's catch except that it bit a worm dangled from a cane pole using the "sneakup" system McKenzie developed to take fish from the crystal waters of Ketona Lake, a small pond in a Birmingham, Alabama, suburb. The pond is posted now by the new owners after several drownings. But kids still sneak in and report 2- and 3-pound bluegills.

McKenzie doesn't have to go back, he's got a strong memory, and a mounted fish, to remind him of that long ago April afternoon in 1947 when he set, but lost the record forever. McKenzie fished Ketona Pond, a quarry pond just five minutes from his home, often before or after his shift at the local bolt and rivet company.

"You could grab some worms, a quill bobber and a cane pole and catch enough bluegills for dinner any day," McKenzie said. "I usually got 15 to 20 bluegills that went between ¾ pound and 1½ pounds. There were a lot of big bass in the little lake, too, but you couldn't catch them very often on bait or lures. After a while, we quit trying for bass after I discovered 'the trick' for bluegills; they came easy.

"The trick was really simple. The water in the ponds was all from seepage. There was no run-off. So it was so clear you could see bottom at 10 feet, easy. Fish would spook if they saw you. So we rigged with no weight and a quill bobber and crawled up to the edge of the bank."

"If you hunkered down real quiet, and stuck the pole out over the water, your gob of worms would sink naturally until it was 4 or 5 feet deep. The quill would lie there flat on the water. When you got a hit, you would watch the quill tip up and follow it down with the tip of the pole until the quill was a couple of feet deep. Then, set the hook." Interestingly enough, this is the exact technique, even to the quill bobber, that British anglers use for their highly sophisticated match fishing for species like bream that much resemble our bluegills.

McKenzie said, "That day I tied on a No. 3 Harrison hook baited with a red worm on some 6-pound-test line, and crawled up to the edge. You had to sneak up on the fish and peek over the edge. They would spook if they spotted you. Cane poles let you catch a lot of fish fast because you could move the bait right to the fish. My friend and I already had about 15 bluegills. It was a pretty slow day, and I wondered if we'd have dinner fish."

His next hit was different! When he hauled back on the

Coke McKenzie poses with the mount of his bluegill that missed being a world record by a mere 2 ounces. This bluegill weighed in at 4 pounds, 10 ounces. He caught it in Ketona Lake, Alabama, in 1950.

pole, the fish didn't come up at all. It dived and circled. "I figured I had a bass," McKenzie said. "I'd lost bass before. I didn't think I'd land him."

McKenzie mentioned a couple of kids out gigging frogs who came up and, while he tried hard not to break off his fish on his 6-pound-test line, kept asking questions. McKenzie never really saw the fish in the water. It was getting dark, the quarry water was shaded and dark and he couldn't see well from his perch over the water.

"Suddenly," he said, the excitement still plain in his voice more than 40 years later, "this monster, the biggest bluegill I'd ever seen, rolled up on his side. There was no way to get him up the steep bank."

Fortunately, McKenzie figured out a way. He talked the two

rubbernecking boys out of a frog gig, jabbed the fish and, now in the dark, headed home.

"It's a good thing I didn't clean the fish," McKenzie said. "We had company at the house, so I left it in the refrigerator in a pan of water. I planned on cleaning it in the morning, but the company stayed late, and I had to rush to work. We got to talking about the fish. The foreman and I got to arguing about its size. Then, my boss heard how big it was. So he sent a man over to the house to get the fish. When the fish was weighed that afternoon, it ran 4 pounds, 10 ounces."

In perspective, this is a blockbuster bluegill. The previous record was only 2 pounds, 8 ounces. Shortly after Coke McKenzie's record, a 3½-pound bluegill came from Ketona Pond. Then, on April 9, 1950, T. S. Hudson caught his still-record 4-pound, 12-ounce fish. McKenzie, when interviewed at age 77 and with a wife in failing health, ruefully commented, "I should have weighed that fish right away. I know it had to weigh at least 5 pounds. I'm sure it was larger than Hudson's fish that got weighed right away. I saw both fish mounted, and mine was bigger." So, instead of holding a record, McKenzie, by waiting 20 hours to weigh his fish, has been second best for over 40 years. While he patiently answers questions and willingly sends photos of his mounted bluegill, you can, if you listen carefully, still hear his sense of loss because of those extra 2 ounces.

Bluegill Bonanza & Bream Breakthroughs

Two record fish in three years from one small pond does seem odd. Alabama fisheries experts wondered what made the Ketona bluegills so big, so they went over for a look. In an October, 1979, *Outdoor Life* article on the record bluegill written by John Phillips, Barry Smith, then assistant Chief of Fisheries for Alabama, noted: "There are two lakes at Ketona, a small lake where the world records were taken and a larger lake that is also supposed to have nice bluegills. But because of the larger lake's steep banks, the little lake was the only one we could get into.

"We tried shocking and other tactics to collect some of the big bluegills, but all we could come up with were average-sized fish. The department wanted some of the Ketona Lake bluegills because we had reasoned that the genetic makeup of these fish might be such that they would foster larger bluegills than we were currently producing at our state hatchery."

Such turned out not to be the case. Environmental factors, and World War II, which took some fishing pressure off the fish, seemed to make the difference at Ketona Lake. Scale checks of McKenzie's bluegill showed it to be nine years old. That is three years older than most experts calculated as a maximum age attainable for a bluegill at that time.

Limestone waters like Ketona's help grow bigger fish, too. As always with panfish, overpopulation, stunting and competition with a large age class keep sizes down. In small Ketona Lake, there were huge numbers of bass to eat smaller bluegills and extremely limited spawning areas for bluegills on small limestone ledges. So few bluegills hatched, and most became bass food.

The common situation that pulls bass out of bass and panfish waters until panfish take over, didn't occur. The local people hadn't figured out how to catch the bass in this suburban Birmingham lake.

"The company that bought the site drew down the ponds after fish and game did their study," McKenzie said, "but Ketona Lake filled back up. Now you can't get permission to fish. Kids still tell me that they sneak in and bring out 2- to 3-pound bluegills all the time. So, I guess you could still set a record, if you could get in to fish. With all the fancy gear they have now, somebody might break Hudson's record."

You get the impression McKenzie wouldn't mind being number three on the list, if Hudson were dropped down to number two. It's being second, answering questions about the "second best" bluegill for generations that McKenzie regrets. That, and the hours his "5-pound" bluegill shrank in the refrigerator.

Perspective

Forty years is a long time to hold a record for fish as widely distributed and easily accessible as bluegills. Given the number of potential ponds, lakes, flooded strip mines and other waters across the country, it seems possible that T.S. Hudson's record could eventually be broken. Every fisheries biologist interviewed in the South has stories of record bream that go direct from water to cooking oil.

Nationwide records offer a better perspective for those in other areas. The NFWFHF records top out with a 3-pound, 8-ounce fish taken by Darren May in Illinois. The IGFA records top out with a 4-pound, 3-ounce bluegill caught in 1980 by Phil Moore Conyers in Hopkins County, Kentucky. The last fish suggests that larger specimens may die of old age somewhere. The key is finding the ultimate "honey hole," such as Ketona Pond, where the conditions are ideal to produce those solitary, huge bluegills that break records.

Saltwater Records

21

Bonefish— Phantom Of The Flats

S portsman A. J. McClane, one of America's top fishing authorities, once said, "Like most observers, I have long believed that bonefishermen need a psychoanalyst." You can make a case that anyone who spends much time on the sun-blasted flats that bonefish prefer fails the "Mad dogs and Englishmen" sanity test. A bonefish, like a tarpon, isn't worth eating. They aren't very big. They aren't hard to catch on bait. They don't jump, but, boy do they run—if you give them a chance, that is. Noted fishing writer Philip Wylie once showed that a 6-pound bonefish couldn't break a 6-pound test line if you simply clamped down on the drag and never let the fish run. So why the bonefish mystique?

The surroundings on most flats where bonefish cruise contribute the most to their mystique. While the all-tackle record 19-pound bonefish and many other large bonefish came from deep water off Zululand, South Africa, and off Hawaii, Jack Samson, the well-known saltwater fly fisherman, correctly said, "It's easy to catch bonefish in deep water with bait."

Farming Bonefish

So the reason most specialists chase bonefish is the hunt, and the flats. As is true with rising trout, you spot, stalk and approach these elusive fish. Do everything right, and you have a chance. Flash a rod with an extra back cast, slop line on the water, pitch a lure or bait too close to these reflective fish you spot by their shadow, and all you see is a cloud of mud or puff of sand. Mr. Bonefish has, with better moves than Dr. J., made off into the distance.

Releasing A Record

Local knowledge, like spotting fish, helps in the ever-changing world of the bonefish flats. Even compulsive flats fishermen like Dr. Corky Adams, who has held 21 light-tackle records at one time or another since the 1970s, do best on the flats when they team up with experienced guides. Dr. Adams, a past president of the American College of Chest Physicians, and now in his 70s, still runs triathlons, "to stay in shape for fishing." He specializes in shallow-water, light-tackle action.

He caught the first sailfish taken on 2- and 4-pound test. In 1985, he held the 2-pound-test line class records for bonefish, tarpon and permit, the flats fisherman's light-tackle grand slam. Adams counts his days on the flats in the thousands since he started catching bonefish in the 1940s, but each day, and each fish, is special.

Dr. Adams set the 2-pound line class record on Labor Day weekend in 1984 with an 11-pound, 12-ounce bonefish. He also holds the 2-pound line class record permit with a 25-pound, 7-ounce fish. He took both fish with guide Steve Huff out of a Huff-designed skiff that's popular with many other guides who pole the flats. Dr. Adams also sticks with a Steve Huff rod, Daiwa reel and Ande 2-pound-test line.

The record day, as happens, hadn't started well. As Dr. Adams remembers, "I wanted to get out on the flats for some quiet. (Dr. Adams has 12 children, and with spouses and grandchildren, holidays mostly mean a full house.) So I met Steve and we headed out early. I wanted to try to get my 2-pound line class tarpon record back. Steve found a super spot where there was no way a tarpon could cut the light line off. The conditions were perfect and I hooked a nice 80- or 90-pound tarpon right off." (The 2-pound line class record then was much lower than the current 54-pound standard.)

Dr. Adams continued, "We went back and forth across this big flat after the fish. Steve would pole me up close so I could play the fish off the doubled line. Then the tarpon would dart away. We'd follow. This went on for two and a half hours.

Crawford W. Adams holds the 11-pound, 12-ounce bonefish that he caught in 1984 at Islamorada, Florida. It was big enough to become the IGFA's 2-pound line class record.

Since the tarpon couldn't leave the shallow spot at that tide stage we had the fish belly-up and licked barely out of reach at the boat.

"I turned to Steve and said, 'Nothing else can happen.' The tarpon started sinking under the boat. Then, sort of casually, he swam to the side. When he did, he barely touched the line to the push pole Steve had driven into the bottom to hold the boat. The line just went slack. Steve laid down in the boat and said, 'My God, when are you going to learn to fish?' Some days are like that. This one had to get better!

"We decided to switch species to change our luck. Steve had a flat picked out for bonefish. He'd seen a couple of big ones there just two weeks before. Now that the tides had come around again they could be ready. So was I after losing the tarpon," Adams explained, as his recollection continued.

Bonefish—Phantom Of The Flats

Dr. Adams had rigged up with his special bonefish rod, a Steve Huff model, a Daiwa reel and Ande 2-pound-test line tied to an IGFA standard leader, and a single hook. As is true with all good flats guides, Huff had sorted through the bait dealer's stock for large and lively shrimp. As Dr. Adams tells it, his record catch seems routine.

"I saw the bonefish's shadow first and pitched my shrimp out in front," he said. "The bonefish picked up the bait, felt the hook and shot off. Steve did most of the work, he poled his heart out in the heat. The fish crossed the flat, circled at some mangroves, came back and, as the tide started to rise, dove over the side of the flat into a cut. Only then did I start to worry. But Steve got up to the fish before it could cut us off. I got the double line back on the reel and that was that."

This becomes matter-of-fact only after many records. Dr. Adams remarked about catching a world record bonefish and releasing it "just before the Islamorada tournament when I thought I could catch it again on the same flat. That didn't work." He also remarks on the "thousands of bonefish he has caught and released over the years. Dr. Adams has also won the Islamorada bonefish contest three times, and has caught two bonefish over 14 pounds, four of five over 13 pounds. Still, he would rather talk about fish landed and lost, than about his many records.

Mostly, he talks about the flats with wonder clear in his voice, "It's never the same. Different fish, different weather, different light, but it's always a quiet place to get away. I definitely like that."

Fun On The Flats

So, clearly it's really "the flats" that make bonefish special. Florida's flats still offer unique fishing habitat and fine fishing a short drive from fishermen who trailer boats down to Islamorada and the other islands along the causeway to Key West. Christmas Island, Belize and more remote areas grow in popularity with the "cost no object" angler. Expert Florida fishing guides insure quality catch and, mostly, release action on the miles of shallow, sandy or muddy water that shimmers calm reflections of the sun.

Bonefish, the "ghosts" of the flats, are barely visible to

skilled eyes as they drift across the shallows. Permit, an even more treasured catch that, with bonefish and tarpon, make up a "flat's grand slam" fin by. Barracudas pivot to keep their heads pointed toward poled skiffs and wading fishermen. Sharks move into the shallows. Mullet jump. It's a magic place accessible to any angler, for fishermen need neither fancy tackle nor sophisticated techniques to catch "bones."

As with other "mythical" species, like grayling, reality does not always come up to literary accounts. For example, much of the literature insists that bonefish are difficult to take. Most of this is written by those who insist on using fly rods or lures. Even so, Jack Samson, in *Line Down! The Special World Of Big-Game Fishing*, tells of a day when he fished with the noted angler A.J. McClane. McClane rigged up a 6-inch-long yellow floating plug.

Samson asked, "What you after with that?"

"Oh, anything," A.J. said in his maddening casual manner. "Lots of fish will take a plug on the flats—tarpon, jacks, barracuda, bonefish."

"Bonefish, on that thing," Samson said.

McClane didn't bother to answer, but twitched the big plug a couple of times and the lure disappeared in a boil of water. The casting reel shrieked as the fish headed southeast.

"That bonefish should go about 8 pounds," said McClane who handed the rod to his wife, Patti. When she landed the fish, it weighed just a bit over 8 pounds.

McClane gave the plug to Samson, who fished it for a couple of hours and caught five barracuda, but no bonefish. Samson put the plug on the wall of his den to keep him from forgetting again that an angler never gets smart enough to know it all.

Rigging For Records

Fishermen do need to be smart enough to rig correctly for flats action and record attempts. Experts who use light line try to fight fish "off the double line," a section that connects the line to the leader.

On 2-pound-test outfits, for example, the double section of 2-pound line connects to a short section of 4-pound test, then to 20-, 30- and, for tarpon or other fish with abrasive bodies,

50- and even 80-pound test tippet. See IGFA rules.

Run Shallow, Run Fast

A proper leader helps keep bonefish from abrading the line on coral or mangroves on long runs. For there is no question that bonefish scoot once they fin a full head of steam up. They run like hyperthyroid carp. Given the size, and the speed of the sharks on the flats, this is a survival necessity. Dr. Adams mentioned watching a lemon shark chase a bonefish so fast that both fish beached and had to flop and wiggle back into swimming depths.

Still, it's important that fishermen realize that catching bonefish, jacks and other species on the flats doesn't need to bust the family bankroll. It does pay to invest in a good guide—even a half-day booking can teach the basics. Beginners can catch fish from the start if they follow directions and, mostly, use bait and take fish as they come. For bonefish share the flats with huge tarpon, the very elusive permit and an assortment of other species. So there is always something to watch in the shallow water.

22

The Great Whites

Australians have had a love-hate relationship with sharks ever since Captain Bligh beat sharks away from his long boat after being set adrift by *Bounty* mutineers. As the largest island in the world, Australia has plenty of shoreline—most of which seems well-stocked with sharks. Beaches feature shark nets, flags and warning sirens. Tourists flock to buy shark-tooth jewelry. Lifeguards keep a shark watch, hoist flags and close beaches when the great whites and other dangerous species cruise, fin out, just beyond the shore breaks. So Australians are always interested in reducing the shark population by whatever means. In the past, this has led to some problems with the IGFA because lines heavier than 130-pound-test are not allowed.

Alf Dean met IGFA standards with a huge 2,664-pound record "great white" caught off Ceduna, a quiet coastal town popular with tourists in South Australia. The huge shark, taken during the Australian "winter" on April 21, 1959, remains the IGFA white shark all-tackle record set on 130-pound test, or 39-thread line. Dean's catch decisively smashed the 2,350-pound, 39-thread record held by Bob Dyer, a well-known Australian radio personality. It was Dean's fourth time in succession to have held the all-tackle record Australian-style. One of these fish, a 2,536-pound monster caught on super stout 54-thread line, didn't qualify for IGFA status, since the line used was over the 130-pound test limit.

Dean first took the all-tackle record in Streaky Bay toward Adelaide from Ceduna; then broke it there the following year. He then broke his Streaky Bay record at Ceduna. In the meantime, Dyer grabbed Dean's 130-pound shark record. Anxious to regain his lost record, Dean had spent 10 days searching for monster sharks in Ceduna waters with his skipper, (Australians call them "boatmen," a more descriptive term) Ken Puckridge. They had not seen a single shark. Big gamefishing can be like that even in an area where there are at least 10 different species that include gummy, school, bronze whaler, hammerhead and many more. "The bigger the fish, the longer the wait" seems an international rule!

Given this, and the fact that Point Sinclair, just down the coast, boasts of white, unspoiled beaches with a shark-proof swimming enclosure, it's rather amazing that nearby Cactus Beach is famous for its powerful right and left-hand breaks that attract summer surfers from all over Australia.

Of course, Aussie surfers see sharks something like jay-walkers see automobiles, as a moving hazard to avoid; like swimmers and skin divers, they need to take care in Australian waters. Rodney Fox, from Adelaide, knows about this. He sports 400 stitches after a great white attack!

Dean almost didn't fish the night he hooked his last record. He had packed up most of his tackle and was ready to leave for home. With his vacation winding down, he and his boatman decided to stay out all night and try one more time off Bird Rocks just to catch some snapper to take home to eat. About 3:30 in the morning, the big shark bumped their boat as it swirled past after a hooked bottom fish. They had some chum aboard so they poured blood and oil into the water.

The big shark, its dorsal fin cutting though the surface a la' the movie *"Jaws,"* circled the boat, then disappeared. They thought they had lost the fish, but it came back into range. Only a careful husbanding of chum with periodic waiting periods kept the big fish in the area until daybreak. It's simply too dangerous to try and land a great white during the night,

At about 7 a.m., Dean slung his big bait over the side of the boat. The fish bit immediately, and took off down the coast. They followed as Dean constantly varied pressure on his line, and his boatman changed angles to keep the big fish off balance

This white shark which weighed in at 2,664 pounds is the IGFAs's all-tackle record as well as the record for the 130-pound line class. It was caught by Alf Dean off of Ceduna, Australia, in 1959.

The Great Whites

and working. No rest here. Only steady pressure would do the job. Then, too, given the number of other sharks possibly in the area, a quick fight and a quicker trip back to hoist the shark safely out of the water was a must. Zane Grey, for example, fishing in the Pacific, lost a marlin record when sharks took one huge bite out of his fish at the boat.

The experienced pair showed their teamwork. They only took 50 minutes to bring the monster shark alongside the boat where it was gaffed and tail-roped for the haul back to the weighing station. "A good boatman makes a big difference," Dean said. "We were able to work the fish all the time without too much line out. The fight wasn't that hard. I did worry a bit when the fish jumped. It's something to see such a big fish slam back into the water after jumping clear."

Dean's monster did this twice before they could sink gaffs and tail-rope their catch for the tow back to Denial Bay just 14 kilometers from Ceduna. It boggles the mind to consider the situation if a green shark jumped into the boat!

As the huge fish Australians call a "white pointer" was weighed on the official scales at Denial Bay jetty, hundreds of sightseers, surfers and vacationing fishermen trying their luck off the rocks for swimmer crabs, jammed the jetty and docks. Some winter surfers were glad not to be sharing the water with this "great white." As rubberneckers mobbed the weight station, the huge shark pulled the balance beam down to 2,664 pounds. It stretched 16 feet, 10 inches in length and its girth was nearly 10 feet. Dean had his record back.

Mundus' Montauk Monster

Chumming with a whale isn't exactly what IGFA had in mind when they laid out the rules for international angling records. So it may be a good thing that, in the *Sports Illustrated* coverage of "The One That Didn't Get Away" the text noted that Frank Mundus, then 60 years old and the grizzled, real-life model for the Quint Character in *"Jaws,"* hooked the fish, and his partner, Donnie Braddick, played the monster for nearly two hours. The line test, described at various times as 130-pound test, 150-pound test or even 200-pound test, wasn't exactly what you might expect IGFA to allow. They accept 130-pound test tops. So it's no surprise that this "record" remains unofficial and unrecognized by the IGFA.

However, 3,450 pounds is a lot of shark to catch on anything short of power winches. It's too bad the planning didn't match the execution! Especially since Mundus insists the shark caught that day was only the second largest they saw!

Both fishermen are professional fishing skippers. They had left Montauk, New York, August 4 in their boats on overnight charters. With calm seas, they looked for bluefin tuna. Mundus located one, but it refused the bait. So Mundus kept going because he wanted to give the party some extra time, and he had no bookings that night. Braddick spotted Mundus, ran up alongside, and told him about a dead whale he had found about 25 miles off Montauk.

Braddick knew Mundus wanted to catch a shark like Dubrule's "Ralph" on rod and reel. So, after some discussion, both boats headed for the floating and, by this time, very smelly whale. Several hours later, Braddick's party took a blue shark. After more waiting, punctuated by some walking about on the floating, bloated whale by macho mates and others who apparently had not seen *"Jaws"*, Mundus and Braddick's parties, after 24 hours out, had enough blue water for the time being. So Mundus tied up onto the whale with his running lights on to wait. Braddick took both parties of tired fishermen back to Montauk, made a fuel and pizza stop and got back out to the giant floating carcass about midnight. Braddick tied up to Mundus' boat that was still attached to the whale.

After nearly 24 hours looking for fish and, one suspects, a fill of pizza and something to drink, both skippers dozed off. At 2:30 a.m., mate John Dileonardo woke the skippers with news of the first great white. They weren't thrilled. You don't mess with great whites after dark. They voted to wait for dawn and went back to sleep.

The next morning more sharks had gathered. At times, six circled the dead whale. Mundus started to tease the sharks into a feeding frenzy. During this time, the skippers had named the individual sharks. Mate John Dileonardo got the first chance, but lost the estimated 2,000-pounder after 20 minutes when the shark sheered a ⅛-inch stainless steel cable leader that Mundus claimed "couldn't be cut with pliers."

After carefully rigging up with another huge bait, Mundus

tried to get "The Big One," the largest of the sharks that now moved in to tear bucket-size pieces of blubber from the bobbing whale. Instead, "White Tip," a smaller fish, engulfed the bait. Braddick, who was on the rod, said, "It felt like a freight train. The first time the fish came up he thrashed around only about 25 feet from the boat. The second time he stayed about 50 feet behind the boat and came right at us. The third time he was rolled up in the leader and way out of the water with his pecs (pectoral fins) spread, flapping his jaws in slow motion. It was awesome. My line was actually going up!"

Mundus began to get nervous as the fight wore on into its second hour. Then, after an hour and three-quarters, he decided to end it. He slammed the boat into reverse and backed down on the fish until a mate could grab the wire leader. What the mate thought about all this never came out. One can imagine how it felt to grab a wire leader and try to drag a fish nearer that weighed over a ton and a half, and could, with one bite, chop a man into two tasty sections.

After a struggle, and more hands on the wire, Dileonardo stuck in a big gaff. A second gaff slammed into the frantic shark. Then, a head choker and tail rope secured the fish to the side of the boat, and they took off for home before the other sharks could attack their trussed prize. It was time to let the folks on shore know what was coming in.

At the dock, mobs of tourists gathered with memories of the "Jaws" movie. Television, newspaper and radio interviewers flocked around Mundus and Braddick. The huge fish weighed 3,427 pounds and was 17 feet long. Mundus, even though Braddick had reeled in the fish, had finally caught the largest fish ever taken on rod and reel from his boat.

However, most of the fuss started when the two skippers tried to get IGFA to certify the record. IGFA, after an investigation, did not. So "Big Daddy," as the fish came to be called locally, isn't listed by the IGFA. It is listed in the *Guinness Book Of World Records*.

23

Budget Tiger Shark Record

W alter Maxwell remembers June 14, 1964, as much for the fish he lost as for the fish he eventually beached. "The big one nearly overlapped the pier's end," he said. "That's 20 feet long." Maxwell's "little" shark only ran 13½ feet in length. After losing an estimated 10 percent of its body weight, it strained the local truck scales for a tiger shark world record 1,780 pounds.

Sharks, all *"Jaws"* propaganda aside, seem the most democratic of predators. They eat dead fish and dead bodies, cardboard boxes and tin cans, Styrofoam and shoes and anything else that crosses their path. So it's only fitting Maxwell's "monster" is the only record "grander" (gamefish over 1,000 pounds on IGFA legal gear) taken from shore rather than an expensive charter craft. Maxwell showed the kind of planning, equipment care, physical skills and, yes, luck, the average fishermen needs to set big fish records without a whale-size bank account.

"Shark fishing was big that summer," Maxwell said. "We could see huge sharks cruising along the shore, and the tiger's stripes showed up clearly from the piers. I thought I knew why more fish were not caught. Even when I lived in North Carolina, I had watched shark fishermen for years. I had noticed that most shark fishermen didn't seem rigged right. Gear was okay for smaller bar sharks, but not for the big tigers.

"I was 34 and strong from carrying bricks in those days. So,

I knew I could set a record. I felt that all I needed for a record was the right equipment and a decent chance."

Budget Big Game Gear

Maxwell geared up with a bargain $135 left-handed 16/0 Penn Senator, a very sturdy classic reel that lacks the refinements of today's high-tech "grinders."

"There wasn't much demand for reels that big then," he said. "Especially left-handers!" Jim Mitchie, who helped gaff the record tiger shark, built Maxwell a custom 39-thread rod from a Shakespeare blank mounted with sturdy double-wrapped Mildrum guides.

"Jim got me started on sharks, and teased me with some big fish," Maxwell said. "I watched big game fishermen on film and knew I needed a harness with a rod butt holder. So M. C. Meetze made me a special harness so I could put more pressure on the fish. The few hundred dollars I invested in gear was 'big money' for a brick layer in those days."

Though monofilament was available, Maxwell loaded his reel with over 1,300 yards of 130-pound-test Dacron. Maxwell thought the sand color, and the abrasion resistance, of this large-diameter line made it perfect for shark fishing on the sandy stand. His catch testifies to his wise choice.

Gradual Improvements

As Maxwell watched, learned and put his outfit together, other fishermen landed, but mostly lost, increasingly larger sharks. Terminal tackle gradually evolved to match the 3- to 10-pound skates (a bat-shaped bottom fish) local pros used as bait to avoid smaller bait-stealing sharks and rays.

Maxwell eventually settled on a terminal rig with two giant 14/0 needle-eye Mustad hooks whipped onto a little less than 30 feet—the IGFA allowance—of steel leader that is swiveled to the main line.

Rigged and ready to go, Maxwell invested his weekends in the quest for the record tiger. He would arrive Friday night, and "put out a bait until it was time to leave Sunday." That particular Friday night Maxwell hit the pier late. He didn't really get set up until Saturday morning when swimmers turned up to brave the blustery day.

Spectators quickly gathered when Walter Maxwell posed with his trophy tiger shark. It had been just weighed in at a monstrous 1,780 pounds. It's an all-tackle record that has stood for well over two decades.

Since the huge baits used (most states ran a foot to a foot and a half long) were too heavy to cast, Maxwell's buddy, Bill Smith, gathered baits from a half-dozen regulars on the pier, and rowed them out a hundred yards or so to deeper water before plopping them over the side. Then, it was time to wait. The sun grew hotter. Waves built as a storm started to blow in. Anglers slept, gossiped and traded fish stories. The sound of country and western music lost its contest with the radio call of Saturday's baseball game.

Fish On!

With a grinding click, Maxwell's heavy rod bent double. Line surged off the reel. Maxwell grabbed his rod, rammed its butt into his harness, levered in the striking drag, leaned back and set the hook. He strained against the pull of the unseen fish that seemed hardly concerned with the bite of the huge 14/0 hooks. An hour passed with the huge shark seemingly unaware of the 130-pound-test Dacron. Finally, the fish moved into gaffing range at the pier, the tiger stripes barely visible in the clear water.

Mitchie jammed his heavy pier gaff into the fish. The shark surged in the broken water where waves swept the pilings. Mitchell's hooks tore free. Now held only by the home-made gaff's sharp steel hook, and Mitchie's grip on the gaff's fiberglass handle, the shark snapped its head and rolled. It slammed Mitchie against the pier rail, and surged away with the next wave. As it swam out to sea, Mitchie's gaff cut a periscope's wake and submerged. Mitchie headed home in order to "rig a better gaff."

Disheartened, but unwilling to give up, Maxwell rested and replayed the fight. Clearly, he thought, he needed to get off the pier to land the fish in the surf.

Storm clouds and rain dampened Saturday night. Fair weather fishermen left the pier. Wet anglers too compulsive to leave swapped stories and shared hamburgers from a local diner. Most slept huddled against the cold and damp in their sleeping bags. Maxwell dozed and thought about his warm, dry bed far away at home.

Early Sunday morning, a school of skates finned through. Enough hit on light gear to "freshen" baits that Bill Smith gathered, then again rowed out and set in deep water 200 yards out from the pier. Anglers stirred. Coffee steamed as fishermen made donut runs as the day warmed. Latecomers straggled in after church. The more secular-minded traded jokes about Saturday night action and those foolish enough to "sleep out in the rain." Only the gulls, and the sounds of kids happily turning blue in the cool early summer surf, interrupted the anglers basking like harbor seals on the pier. Maxwell's thoughts turned to the week's work ahead.

About 11 a.m., Mitchie, now back with his new and improved gaff, hooked a dusky shark. It "only" went 11 feet. Mitchie had learned from Maxwell's fish. So, with Maxwell's help clearing other fishermen's lines over and under his straining rod, Mitchie got down on the sand and beached his shark under the pier. Things settled down. Smaller sand bar sharks worried baits, but none were big enough to be hooked. Pier life dozed as only the ball game disturbed gulls trying to steal bait from nodding fishermen.

Double Trouble

The rasp of a running drag signaled another big-fish hit. "Nick Laney had hooked a tiger about 11 feet long," Maxwell said. "Or maybe the tiger had him. Nick only had a Penn Senator 9/0 and 150 yards of 130-pound-test line over 50-pound-test backing. If the shark got to the backing, it was gone."

Laney had no real chance. With no heavy leader, there was no way to gaff the fish from the pier, but Laney kept fighting. The big tiger dragged Laney up and down the pier. Fishermen pulled lines, moved gear, offered advice and scrambled to avoid the action. Tourists flocked underfoot anxious to photograph the shark. Another shark hit a bait. Then, another bit and buzzed away.

In the confusion, Maxwell didn't see his rod snap down, but he heard the whir of the clicker against his 30-pound drag as he raced to his rod. More sharks hit. A school moved through. Maxwell's shark surged out of the water. The sound of the one-ton shark falling back into the sea momentarily stopped the action like a filmmaker's freeze frame. Then, as Maxwell struggled to fit his rod into his harness, his line went slack. Other sharks broke free as anglers cursed and struggled as their lines crossed to saw each other to frayed destruction.

Maxwell reeled frantically, unsure whether his fish was still hooked. Then, he slammed to the rail. His shark was still on, still pulling as line smoked from the reel. Maxwell braced himself on a fisherman's bench, jammed his feet against the pier rail, locked his arms and put his back to it. The mighty tiger kept running. It was pointless to pump as line peeled off the huge reel.

"My tiger rolled again about 200 yards from the pier," Maxwell said. "It sounded like nothing I'd ever heard." A plumber buddy later reported the splash looked and sounded like "someone had dumped two bathtubs into the ocean at once."

Laney's fish continued its strong fight. Everyone else had

lost their fish. So, anglers gave both fishermen welcome room with their unwanted advice. Maxwell knew Laney couldn't control his fish on his light gear. He worried about crossed lines and snags until Laney's fish ran north along the beach and Maxwell's went south. Laney ran to the end of the pier, jumped 15 feet or so down to the beach and followed his surging shark.

"Last time I saw him he had three dozen tourists behind him and North Carolina in front of him," Maxwell said. "My shark headed toward Florida!" Nick Laney eventually lost his fish when, still somewhat green because of Laney's light gear, it reversed its course, and the line snapped off on mussel-covered pilings under the pier.

Maxwell, neck muscles straining, arms locked, and legs braced against the pier, leaned back and continued to haul on the fish. Nothing affected its run. The huge shark now had nearly a half mile of line out. The nearly-a-mile of line on the huge 16/0 reel continued to run out. Maxwell could feel the grinding vibrations of the shark rubbing along the sand as it finned away from the pier. Tourists gathered as Maxwell's friends tried to cordon off the end of the pier. Maxwell knew he would lose his world record if anyone touched the reel or helped with the fish. Like most of the regulars on the pier he knew the IGFA regulations and thirsted for a record!

With nearly 1,200 yards of line out, the tiger finally slowed. Then, gradually submitting to the pull of the hook and Maxwell's unrelenting pressure, the shark turned. Maxwell cranked slack as fast as possible to regain lost line. The heavyweight fight ebbed and flowed like the "Thrilla in Manila." Line built up on the reel, then smoked off, slowed and stopped. Maxwell grimly pumped it back. Three times the shark jumped. Five times the line slacked as Maxwell wondered if he had lost his fight. Crowds built, and then thinned as the day faded. Maxwell hung on.

The problem was leverage. Maxwell pulled his huge shark up as well as closer to the pier. This worked to the shark's advantage. The shark could use its weight to pull the rod down. The closer the shark got to the pier, the greater its leverage. Even if Maxwell could haul the shark to the pier, if the fish brushed a mussel-covered piling, it would be lost. Tigers, like other sharks, can roll up in leaders, too. The least amount of slack could be fatal. If the sturdy wire leader snagged on the shark, the shark's abrasive skin could abrade even 130-pound Dacron.

Maxwell didn't have any relief. There was no boat to back down to the fish. There was no skilled mate to tell Maxwell what to do or move a fighting chair back. There was no experienced deckhand to wire the fish. Worst, there was no chance to rest against the drag as the boat moved. Maxwell sweated, strained, grunted and hung on. The slightest error and the shark would be in the pilings and lost.

Finally, ever so slowly after four hours and 30 minutes of gut wrenching effort, the huge shark neared the pier. From his perch over the clear water, Maxwell could see the size of his "tiger." He could also see that one of the hooks had been bitten off. Only one hook remained fast in the shark's lip just outside the row of gnashing teeth. Only this hook's placement had insured the long fight. Had it ground home between the tiger's teeth, the shark's multiple rows of triangular teeth would have long since cut it through, and Maxwell off!

With a final desperate surge, Maxwell hauled back on his rod and held his position as the tight drag forced the shark's mouth open. The wire leader drew within reach, but even Andre the Giant couldn't wire a ton of shark from a pier 20 feet above the ocean. Mitchie, his new gaff now "roped" so it wouldn't follow yesterday's gaff out to sea, poised on the rail like a cormorant ready to strike.

Mitchie had to gaff the shark in the corner of its mouth without knocking Maxwell's single remaining hook free. If set anywhere else, his gaff would tear out against the ton weight and thrashing antics of this monster. Mitchie jerked the needle-sharp steel gaff head home. The tiger turned to flee. The gaff pole pulled loose, but its head and line held. Maxwell's buddies were on one end of the inch-thick rope; the shark on the other. The shark thrashed. The rope slipped and burned work-hardened palms. For a time, it wasn't sure who had whom. Then, with a careful sidle to avoid the shark's snapping jaws and rows of crunching teeth, Mitchie waded into the shore break and lassoed the shark's head and tail. It took nearly a dozen men on three stout ropes to drag the huge fish safely above the surf line onto the brown sandy beach.

Mitchie said it first, "That's a record."

Unfortunately, much time passed as the gathering crowd waited for a wrecker's truck to load the huge fish on a flatbed truck for its trip to the truck scales for weighing. The fish spewed up "barrels of seawater, shrimp and partly digested food" as it dehydrated and lost weight. It was finally weighed at 9 o'clock the next morning in nearby Loris. Even so, Maxwell's tiger beat the old record by 350 pounds. If the fish had been quickly weighed, fisheries experts agree it would have topped 2,000 pounds. Today, it stands as the largest fish ever caught from the shore with IGFA standard tackle.

Luck? Perhaps. But it hardly seems an accident that Walter Maxwell caught the North Carolina record 1,150-pound tiger shark a couple of years later. In a recent interview, he said, "I still wonder about the first tiger I hooked. I know it was bigger. Catching the record tiger really went about the way I expected. I guess I was lucky."

Since the South Carolina beach town, where city fathers saw *"Jaws,"* considered tourism and prohibited shark fishing from piers and most beaches, Maxwell's record may never be broken from the shore. Experts agree that tiger sharks that weigh over a ton swim the ocean. Even if one is caught, it will most likely be taken from a specialized big game boat with a professional crew and experienced deckhands. So, nothing can diminish Walter Maxwell's accomplishment. Like "Old Blue Eyes," Frank Sinatra, he did it his way!

24

Blue-Collar Bluefin Tuna

Ken Fraser keeps the tail of his record bluefin tuna in his basement, He "couldn't afford to have it mounted then." Now, with the red meat of bluefin tuna selling for $30 a pound to Japanese buyers who scavenge off Nova Scotia and Prince Edward docks, his 1,496-pound catch would be worth a fortune. Ken Fraser said it didn't bring in much. "I did get some recognition from *Sports Illustrated*. But as far as Canada is concerned, nothing," he said.

A cynic might suggest Fraser was in the wrong place at the right time on his record day. An experienced saltwater guide and lobsterman, Fraser had fished off his boat, the *Astar*, all season out of Prince Edward Island. Then, the big tuna left for Nova Scotia. So Fraser, a Prince Edward Island skipper, caught his record off a friend's Nova Scotia boat in the great Nova Scotian waters.

There does seem a certain friendly malice between these two areas. When Nova Scotia Tourism was called about Fraser's record fish, they responded with a photo and the information that they thought Fraser had died a couple of years ago. As Mark Twain once said, reports of his death were exaggerated.

Only Fraser's interest in fishing has died. For Fraser no longer fishes; he has sold his boat and licenses and now works for an oil company.

As he sorrowfully said, "Prince Edward Island sportfishing is not really any good now, and they only catch a few fish in Nova

Scotia. Bluefin are about the only sportfish, and everyone has gone to harpoons and rope and super-heavy line. Fish are worth too much to lose.

"Besides, the Japanese long-liners are really cleaning out all the brood stock. We probably helped, too. In the 1970s when Elwood Harry and that crowd came up here, we'd put a lot of fish on the dock. One day in the early '70s, we put 49 bluefin on the wharf. I guess we caught too many fish."

Getting the story of the catch from Fraser is a bit like removing shark teeth.

"I don't like to get too involved with records," he said. "Every so often I speak to sports writers. I used to send out pictures, but that costs too much now that the Nova Scotia people don't send me photos. I do sign a few photos for IGFA to auction off at their big thing in Florida, but I'm not into that kind of fishing any longer.

"I don't read very much about records. I know I have the IGFA all-tackle and 130-pound line class records, and I belong to the IGFA 10-to-1 and 1,000-pound clubs. I'm in the *Guinness Book Of World Records*, too."

We do know Fraser set his record on October 26, 1979, while fishing on his friend Captain Eric Samson's boat. Bluefin had left Fraser's favorite grounds off the small hamlet of North Lake on Prince Edward Island about October 15. So, when Samson called Fraser up and invited him to fish if Fraser would bring his chair and gear, Fraser headed right over. Samson, apparently, enjoyed little luck with what turned out to be one of the last big runs of monster tuna before long-liners and overfishing decimated their stocks.

The big tuna were feeding hard in "the causeway," a constricted area Fraser remembers as really congested with a lot of boats. He said it's like a funnel, so the bluefin could gang up on baitfish. It was somewhat like fishing in an aquarium. Boaters probably caught 100 or so fish over about three weeks; then the fish migrated.

Fraser grabbed his gear—rods, gaffs, chair, rigs—and went on over to the action. That's how he happened to be in the chair instead of on the bridge. Fraser favored utilitarian tackle: a Fenwick 130 Class rod, Penn International 130 reel filled with 130-pound-test Garcia Line. He rigged a daisy chain of mackerel

The waters of Aulds Cove, Nova Scotia, Canada, yielded this monster bluefin tuna which tipped the scales at 1,496 pounds. It was caught by Ken Fraser.

Blue-Collar Bluefin Tuna

that they trolled right behind the boat with a Mustad 13/0 hook. These strings of a half-dozen, foot-long mackerel are towed close in. As a rule, one daisy chain is set out from a clip on an outrigger about 20 feet long and trolled about 30 feet back. The second chain bounces in and out of the prop wash close over the stern, maybe 15 feet from the transom. This string has a 13/0 hook buried in the last mackerel. So much for the theory that boat wakes scare fish!

"Fishing was good," Fraser said. "We hooked 13 fish in nine days, caught seven, and lost six. Besides the record fish, I had a 1,340-pounder."

Fraser hooked the big bluefin at 9 o'clock in the morning and remembers the fight as "nothing special." This seems a classic case of Canadian understatement. Fraser said these fish weigh as much as a good-size horse.

"We had a string of mackerel out just 15 feet or so from the stern," Fraser said. "When the big fish hit the whole string disappeared. I saw a dorsal fin first, then the sickle-shape tail.

"It seemed odd to be in the chair rather than on the bridge, but I gimbaled the rods and we got the other daisy chain in. It was a tough fight. The fish tore off several hundred yards of line. I tried to fight the fish and help yell directions to the skipper, too.

"With 130-pound test you need to be in good shape. You haul back with your arms and shoulders even though the harness carries most of the load. Your feet brace your body and supply most of the strength to start pumps. That first long run is tough."

Bill Carpenter, past president of the IGFA who caught more than 100 tuna in his life, used to say, "Stop'em or pop'em." Fraser managed that and was able to apply the continuous pressure that brings big billfish in within the hour.

These first runs are critical. If you keep the pressure on it's possible to land even a record fish within an hour. The least pause, the smallest rest from the cutting pressure of harness into back and cramping hands, can mean hours more work, for big bluefin seem to recover faster than fishermen.

When the runs shorten, the skipper backs the boat down on the fish. As they tire, bluefin thrash their heads from side to side with enough force to lift you half out of your seat. Still, this is a sign the end is near. Soon the mate will have the wire in his hand, and the fight will be over.

Such a fight has been described as like hauling a safe up to the top of a 10-story building, reaching out to touch it, and watching the safe drop back to the first floor. Then, the process repeats and repeats and repeats until it's not always certain if the angler has the fish, or the fish has the angler. It is quite certain that your muscles hurt everywhere, and will continue to hurt for days. Still, big gamefishing isn't all action. Long periods of boredom, punctuated by moments of sheer panic and sometimes hours of grinding physical labor landing a fish describe this sport. No wonder it's most popular with fishermen who don't sweat to earn their daily bread!

While bluefin never come easily, Fraser was physically fit, Samson was experienced and luck, that day, was on their side. The big fish came to the boat in 45 minutes.

When they finally got the gaffs in, the fish was so large, Samson and Fraser couldn't get it into the boat, so they drug the fish around alongside all day. The fish wasn't weighed until 9 or 10 o'clock that night.

"I had been celebrating quite a bit," Fraser said, "and I didn't know how big the fish was until I couldn't get my usual tail rope over the fish's tail. If we had weighed the fish right away, it would have gone over 1,500. Even so I don't think my record will be beaten.

"Things have changed. You don't get much use of 130-pound-test tackle these days. Most of the local skippers are into really heavy gear. A lot of the fishermen come up and charter fish with 80-pound class gear. I don't think that will do it on a record fish. Besides, there just aren't that many really big fish anymore. Too much pressure these days. I see lots of greed and jealousy, too. I'm glad I'm out."

Fraser then asked about possible endorsements or show appearances, but didn't seem very disappointed when told the fishing industry was in a down cycle. One gets the impression that his big fish, aside from the check he got from the fish broker, had taken him from great expectations to deep disappointment. It seems even sadder that such wonderful fish are nearly gone and without stronger international limits on their catch, may never return.

Historical Bluefin

For the first couple of hundred years in U.S. history, bluefin were harpooned. Bluefin tuna caught with rod and reel got big gamefishing started in the 1890s. By 1899, when Col. C. P. Morehouse took a 251-pound tuna off California's Catalina Island, there was already the Catalina Tuna Club, the prototype for today's upscale clubs and organizations that set rules for "gentleman's conduct" and "sporting tackle." The CTC was the site of many firsts, such as the first broadbill swordfish, a 355-pounder, taken on rod and reel by William C. Boschen.

The Hemingway Connection

Writer Ernest Hemingway would have appreciated Boschen's fish. Hemingway first saw tuna in Vigo, Spain, in 1921 when he was watching the harbor waters. He said he saw tuna as long as a man that leaped clear of the water and fell again with a noise like horses jumping off a dock. However, he didn't really get to fish for pelagic fish until he moved to Key West in 1931. It wasn't until 1935 that Hemingway first visited Bimini—he was more in tune with Cuban marlin fishing, where he had held the record, a 468-pound fish. When marlin turned up off Bimini, Ernest Hemingway started to fish there, too. He did set an indelible record of a sort; he caught the first two tuna brought whole into Bimini while fishing from his famous boat, the *Pilar*. They only weighed 310 and 381 pounds, and to Hemingway's regret, his friend, Kip Farrington, quickly broke his record. "Papa" got him back when he later cabled Farrington's wife, who took the first broadbill swordfish off the South American Coast, with, "Perfection! The real record is to take the first one, because if you catch the biggest fish, someone eventually is going to catch a bigger one."

25

Black Marlin— Glassell's Granders

lfred Glassell's 1,560-pound record black marlin didn't get to co-star with Spencer Tracy in the film, "The Old Man And The Sea," but its fight, on the day Glassell set the then and some say, "forever" black marlin record, deserved to be filmed for all time. Glassell's fish jumped 49 times. Had this been a bull fight, the crowd would have waved white hankies and set the huge fish free. Instead, it's mounted and on exhibit at the Smithsonian Institution in Washington, D.C., in the Hall of Sea Life.

The "Grander" Time

Between the founding of the International Game Fish Association before World War II and 1990, there were only 143 members who had caught fish big enough to join the 1,000-pound club. Alfred C. Glassell, Jr., became a member with the still world record 1,560-pound black marlin caught off Cabo Blanco, Peru, in August 1953. This was the biggest "grander blitz" ever. At least 38 black marlin that were over 1,000 pounds were taken off Cabo Blanco in just four years. Glassell took four "granders" between 1952 and 1954, and Mrs. Charles E. Hughes caught the women's 130-pound line class 1,525-pound black marlin record.

Today, with improvements in gear and considerable depletion of black marlin stocks resulting from red tides off Peru and long-line attrition everywhere, most of the black marlin records come from Cairns, Australia. The many early Cabo Blanco records molder in old editions of IGFA Annuals. Such seems a shame, for the period, and the place, and Mr. Glassell's "granders" reflect the uniqueness of this period in the history of billfishing. Glassell made the most of a time when tackle and boats had improved enough to make new records possible, but not so much that a skipper and mate could long drop a bait to gut hook, or choke a fish with a huge bait, and then back down and wire green fish for even the most unskilled angler.

The Cabo Blanco Fishing Club

This was a time of big fish and big budgets for those who had the time, money and inclination to battle them off the Peruvian coast. A time when "the right sort" of fishermen from the world over cheerfully paid their $5,000 each to build the Cabo Blanco Fishing Club. They brought boats in from Nova Scotia. They had custom craft, the *Pescador Dos, Petrel* and, for Houston resident Glassell, the *Miss Texas,* designed to Kip Farrington's standards to brave the rough waters off Peru. Club members hired Atlantic Coast skippers to train the local crews.

These efforts opened what were then the world's best sport fishing grounds, before they were largely overrun by commercial long-liners. For Glassell, the early days at the Cabo Blanco Fishing Club were a short time to set long-time records, with perhaps but 200 days on the water spread over several years of March, April and August visits.

The Deeps Of Cabo Blanco

Just how good were these deepwater grounds where the Andes plunged into the Pacific off Peru in the great days? Before the area opened to big gamefishing with three imported sportfishing boats in 1951, the largest fish ever taken was a 976-pound fish caught off New Zealand in 1926. By 1955, when Hemingway visited the area to shoot stock footage for the classic movie *"The Old Man And The Sea,"* there had been 30 black marlin caught that weighed over 1,000 pounds, and three over 1,500 pounds. This came about in four years with only three boats fishing from time to time.

Hemingway had a trip that "was good in spots." He caught 750-, 680- and 910-pound black marlin. Some of this action was filmed by, reports indicate, a crew of lubberly cameramen that reduced Papa to a near rage. One of these pilgrims was on a boat with a Peruvian fisherman who was fighting a near-record striped marlin. A member of the camera crew reached out with a knife and cut the line with the comment, "striped marlin are no good. We don't want them." It's a good thing he didn't do that to Hemingway. Hemingway used to tote a Thompson submachine gun to shoot sharks "and other vermin." It's certain that he was the only vice president of the conservative International Game Fish Association ever to pack a Thompson! Considering the crews, it's no surprise that little of the footage from this expedition made the movie. So Glassell's record black marlin became the star of the *"Old Man And The Sea."*

Glassell's marlin was but one of a huge number of billfish drawn to the area by the rich sea life just off the steep underwater shoreline. Because of a mix of upwelling nutrients and the cold Humboldt Current, billions of sardines, anchovy and other baitfish fed pelagic gamefish and supported millions of sea birds.

Glassell The Man

Alfred J. Glassell was one of the show's stars. He was an important member of a group that included names like Du Pont, Firestone, Knox and Hutton—which developed the Cabo Blanco Fishing Club. In the 1950s, he was, according to Kip Farrington, the well-known fishing writer of the time, "truly the rod-and-reel Young Man of the Sea." Farrington, who also held the black marlin record at one time, linked up with and fished with both Hemingway and Glassell.

Glassell's Records

When Alfred Glassell took a 1,025-pound black marlin off Cabo Blanco, it was a sensation in the press, for it was not just a world record. It was the first black marlin caught that weighed over 1,000 pounds. Glassell soon lost his record to Tom Bates, one of the top fishermen of the era, who took a 1,060-pound black marlin off Cabo Blanco while Glassell was on the way down to fish. Only 17 days later, Glassell regained it with a 1,090-pound black marlin. Glassell also took record big-eye tuna and 20 odd-striped marlin in a single month. The same year Glassell led the American fishing team at the Wedgeport tuna tournament in Canada, and boated a 785-pound tuna.

Glassell was also the only man in the early 1950s to take the four major blue-water species—black marlin, blue marlin, broadbill swordfish and tuna—weighing over 600 pounds. He had more broadbill swordfish (27) than any other fisherman of his time.

Glassell's Record

During his record blitz at Cabo Blanco, Glassell had nine black marlin strikes in 18 days. He boated eight fish that ran 878, 746, 911, 900, 755, 620 and 532 pounds. Then, on August 4, 1952, he met the fish Farrington called, the "Old Man of the Sea." Rigged with a Cero mackerel and spoon, Glassell trolled up his fish with a Tycoon rod, Fin-Nor reel and Ashaway 39-thread (130-pound-test) line. The fish hit the bait. Glassell fed line and waited for the black to return, pick the bait up, run a bit, turn and then swallow the bait. After a long drop back and wait that can seem like hours to the man in the chair, but lasts only 10 to 15 minutes, Glassell slammed the hook in as his boat surged forward.

The huge fish greyhounded off in and out of the water like a small sailfish. In total, it jumped 49 times. Glassell kept the line short and the pressure on. As his boat backed down on the fish hard, waves broke in over the stern at times. By now the captain, crew and Glassell were a smooth team ready for any surprise. So, as the fish jumped itself to exhaustion, it took only an hour and 45 minutes to boat the fish that later weighed in as a 1,560-pound, all-tackle record.

26

Pacific Blue Marlin Record

Pacific blue marlin have been special fish ever since Zane Grey caught the first member of the 1,000-pound Club, a superb fish that weighed 1,040 pounds, off Tahiti in 1930. While the IGFA, after its later formation, disqualified this fish because it was bitten around the tail when at the boat, that fish remains that important first that nobody can ever duplicate. Just how tough "granders" were on the tackle of the time is demonstrated by the fact that it took until 1952 to take another on rod and reel.

Still, while few things beat the excitement of the first hookup to a big billfish, those who insist on catching fish need extreme patience, and cash! According to a National Marine Services study, it "takes an average 10 days of trolling to take a blue marlin."

Adequate All-Tackle

Today, the all-tackle record belongs to Jay William deBeaubien, an affable San Francisco Bay-area yacht broker, who fishes one week a year with Hawaiian captain Bobby Brown. He set his record near Kaaiwi Point off Kona on the big island of Hawaii on May 31, 1982. The catch, taken on 130-pound-test Erskine K-type monofilament line, a Fin-Nor 130 two-speed reel, Erskine rod, and a 400-pound-test monofilament leader, hit a small peanut Kita blue and silver lure. Jay deBeaubien, a very experienced heavy-tackle fisherman, had fished with skipper Bobby Brown for almost 10 years.

On the record day, they were joined on Brown's 43-foot Merritt, *No Problem*, by an Australian mate, Doug Haig, who had wired a great many 1,000-pound fish off Australian reefs. Those who "wire" billfish by seizing leaders in gloved hands have to be tough enough to hold on until gaffs are sunk or, as it usually is the case with smaller fish today, the fish are tagged and released.

The boat ran at a fast troll 16 knots off the lava flows as deBeaubein remembers. "It was going UFO to the grounds" when the big fish hit," he said.

"The fish dragged me back to the transom before I could get set in the chair," he continued. "The fish jumped completely clear of the water twice, and zoomed off several hundred yards of line. I had the reel cranked up to a 40-pound drag setting so we got the fish in sight of the boat in about 15 minutes. Then, things stalled. I'd get the double line on the reel, and then lose it. We kept short on the fish the whole time after the first run."

It took 43 minutes for this smoothly working team to land the fish. At 1,376 pounds, his catch put deBeaubien in the moderately exclusive "10 to 1" club that IGFA uses to give special attention to fishermen who catch fish 10 times their line test. It's too bad deBeaubien waited too long to join Marlin International. Had he been a member he would have cleared $9,000 in prizes for the big fish. As it was, deBeaubien hasn't even seen his fish since it hung on the dock. Apparently, it was to be mounted gratis and returned to skipper Bobby Brown to display, but it got lost in the works. "A guy who owns the Squid Co. in Los Angeles has the fish," deBeaubien said. "He bought it from somewhere. I do know there is a full-size bronze sculpture of the fish done by Kent Olbert at the Broadwalk Condominiums Complex in Brownsville. Haven't seen that either." At this point, deBeaubien's record is a nice workman-like record unlikely to stand up for too long as techniques improve.

Billfishing's All-Time Record

Kelley Everette's Pacific blue marlin is, without question, one of the two or three outstanding billfishing records of the modern era. Everette took his 1,103½-pound Pacific blue

Kelley Everette notched the men's IGFA 30-pound line class record with this 1,103-pound, 8-ounce Pacific blue marlin taken off of Kona, Hawaii, in 1987.

Pacific Blue Marlin Record

marlin on 30-pound test! This experienced light-tackle expert's fish ran 37 times his line test. To catch a fish like this, there can be no mistakes, no tackle problems and no errors of any sort. A "grander" unless kept off balance at all times could pop 30-pound-test line with a single shake of its head.

Everette made no mistakes that Thursday, June 25, 1987. His best move may have been keeping his wife, Jocelyn, off the boat. She holds the women's Pacific blue marlin record for 30-pound test at 639 pounds, the 12-pound line test women's halibut record that's more than 20 pounds heavier than the men's record, and several others including a yellowfin tuna record that took her 10 hours to crank within gaffing range on 16-pound-test line. But she stayed home that day.

Everette had a good crew aboard. Deckhands Dom Fagundes and Scott Davidson were quite experienced, but experienced skipper Carl Schloderer was running Everette's Merritt for the first time. The *Northern Lights*, Everette's classic 37-foot Merritt, is a Bristol (perfect) restoration that took nearly a year. It's smaller and more agile than larger boats used for billfishing further offshore in potentially stormy waters. You don't need a big boat for Kona billfishing as much of the action is in the protected lee of Hawaii's two massive volcanoes.

You do need an agile boat, and perfect coordination between angler and skipper. Only by working the fish, varying the angles and constantly changing the pressure can a big fish come to gaff on light gear. Many experts claim the skipper is 75 percent of the fight, as the boat, properly used, can put on more pressure than the fisherman. This time, this was not the situation, as Kelley Everette had to direct the skipper who wasn't used to the foibles of the Everette boat.

The mate and deckhands have their jobs, too. They brace the angler's swiveled chair with its gimbaled rod holder and help wire and gaff the fish. They can touch neither gear nor line after the fish is hooked. When the fish is in close, the deckhand normally "wires" the fish by hauling in on the leader while the mate plants one and usually more gaffs to pull the fish into the boat. However, in most cases, smaller fish are released, often with tags and only record specimens are kept.

They had left Honokohau Harbor just up the coast from Kona early and headed south on a reasonably calm day. They hit the VV—buoy area first. Several hours and several miles later, Everette hooked a marlin estimated at between 300 and 400 pounds, but lost it.

They moved about and raced back to the VV-buoy. Everette was later asked why he didn't fish the C-buoy that was normally more productive. He replied, "Something told me VV was the spot."

At VV, Everette caught a nice, 3-pound skipjack tuna and rigged it for use as bait. With about 250 feet of 30-pound test out, the crew made a first pass at the buoy. Dom Fagundes, the mate, noticed the bait seemed rather nervous, pulling and darting on the line like it had sensed a bigger fish.

Everette took it easy; with this technique, the angler watches the birds and waits for a hit. Some sit in the chair with the rod gimbaled and ready. With multiple lines out, rods are in holders that must be grabbed and gimbaled while the fisherman attaches his shoulder harness to the reel.

The deckhand, or more usually the mate, holds the line at a mark until he detects a fish. At this point, 10 to 15 feet of loose lines "dropped back" so the quarry fish has time to grab and turn the bait before it is swallowed head first.

On this day, Everette was out of the chair when the blue hit, but as soon as Dom released the line he was back in, harness attached, and ready to go with just enough drag set to control the slack. Schloderer backed the boat down on the fish to shorten the line and insure a better hook set.

Note: Big game reels, like the Penn International Everette used, have quadrant breaking so the drag can be moved by the fisherman during the fight. With a 30-pound-test line, the preset mark might be 10 pounds—effective drag increases as spool diameter decreases on long runs. With a fish near the boat just out of reach, drag might be raised to 14 or 15 pounds plus whatever pressure the fisherman can put on the reel with both thumbs.

Everyone waited to see if the unseen fish would drop or take the bait. Then, as the line came tight, Everette hauled back on the rod, screamed "Forward" at Schloderer, and set the hook as the engines surged.

"Nothing much happened," Schloderer said. "I thought it was a small fish we usually call 'rats.' The fish turned out to sea.

I followed. Kelley kept me working hard. None of us thought the fish would top the one we'd lost earlier."

For an hour and a half, Everette varied the pressure. He kept on Schloderer to constantly change the angle of line to the fish, and to back down on the fish to keep the line short. Every now and then, Everette would use the slack line release maneuver that Mrs. Marron had used to take her big swordfish off the coast of Chile more than 30 years before.

With such smooth teamwork, the fish never got deep and was rarely more than 50 or 100 feet from the boat. This, plus a combination of short and long pumps by the angler, wears out a big fish fast. But there can be no letup, no pauses; big fish recover faster, about five times faster than fishermen who rest. According to Schloderer, "Kelley never let up. He kept the pressure on for the whole fight. Incredible."

Gradually, the combination of skilled angler, quickly reacting skipper and agile Merritt wore the marlin down. The double line section—limited to 30 feet by IGFA regulations —came back until it touched the rodtip. Then, it inched down the roller guides on the custom rod that Tom Green had built in Florida. The swivel between the double line and the final 10 feet of leader popped through the wave. Kelley clamped down on the reel with both thumbs. Kelley and Dom tensed as they saw the fish for the first time.

Suddenly, it charged away. Kelley thought he'd broken the line just as he realized that the fish was not the 700-pound marlin they expected. This fish was huge!

The line went slack as the monster marlin jumped once, twice, three times as it showed silver and blue against the cruel black lava of the volcanic coast. Now, everyone knew they had a huge fish. They hoped for a record. The fish came closer.

The line tightened. Kelley started screaming, "It's a world record. It's a world record." They knew it was bigger than the 626-pound record. Aroused, somewhat alarmed by the near miss, but ready to go, the team focused on the struggle. Kelley pumped the fish up until the leader was almost in reach; then, locking his thumbs to maximize pressure on the 30-pound-test Ande line, hauled. Dom Fagundes leaned out of the boat to grab the leader.

He snatched it with one hand, then the other, with a

In October, 1988, Jocelyn Everette landed this 639-pound Pacific blue marlin which is a women's IGFA 30-pound line class record. It was taken off of Kona, Hawaii.

smooth heave so the fish would ease into range of Scott Davidson's gaff.

"Scott probably saved our record," Everette said. "We had two or three small gaffs rigged and ready, but he had readied the big fish gaff." Scott jammed in the big gaff, then two more. The fish ripped away from the two smaller gaffs, but the big gaff held. Schloderer, for the first time in the nearly two-hour fight, left the bridge and helped set a second large gaff. Then, the crew opened the transom door, and sweated the fish into the teak cockpit. Its tail still stuck out past the transom (and classic Merritts have big cockpits)!

Dom Fagundes knew it was a "grander." Everette, overwhelmed by the fight, thought the fish ran about 700 pounds, enough for a world record. Fagundes had helped land a 1,649-pound marlin so he had a better idea of length-to-weight ratios.

Carl Schloderer turned the boat, cranked up and raced back for the IGFA scale. They called ahead with news of their catch. So, IGFA's Phil Parker, photographers and the news media were at the dock. Parker, known for his pranks, had set the balance beam at 626 pounds, the old record. The beam flipped up. Then he moved the weight to 726 pounds. Then 826, 926 and finally 1026 before the beam even started to become level. The fish finally weighed in at 1,103½ pounds or more than 37 times the line test.

Everette had earned his record. Some lucky fishermen take a half-day charter and luck into a record fish that they barely manage to land with the help of a skilled skipper, good deckhands and a mate willing to wire green fish, and much luck. Everette had worked for his fish. He started billfishing by getting skunked more than 10 times in a row. After he got hooked, he moved from a 22-foot boat through a 27-foot Topaz to a total restoration of his marvelous 37-foot Merritt. He had learned a lot in those years; not all of it on the ocean. Everette was definitely a very tough, super-fit 30-year-old when he caught his record marlin. Logic would suggest he should have been an invalid. He had also been crushed so badly in an accident on the Alaskan pipeline that his right hand was cut off at the wrist, his pelvis shattered—according to Jay deBeaubein, he later lost a leg—and only after subzero temperatures, three days of surgery and 86 pints of blood, did he recover his hand and, after two years in the hospital, his life.

So Kelley Everette stands for more than a "mere" record. He celebrates the human condition and that sheer desire, guts if you like, that make almost anything possible.

=27=

The Marrons' Marvelous Swordfish

Lou and Eugenie Marron once held five swordfish records. Today, only Marron's 1,182-pound all-tackle record and Mrs. Marron's 772-pound, 80-pound line class records remain. Records are like that, made to be broken. In the haste to catch bigger fish, only the perspective of the past puts records in their proper place. Some of the finest records drop out of IGFA or NFWFHF categories. For example, Lou Marron's all-tackle record was, when caught, the biggest gamefish, except shark, ever taken on rod and reel. He also landed the greatest combined weight of fish—two monsters—on one day. This happened after a massive heart attack at age 37 that sent him fishing.

Mrs. Marron's records are equally outstanding. She was the first woman to catch a tuna off the U.S. coast. She set the women's 20-, 30- and 50-pound line test striped marlin records on a day when she caught a total of five marlin. She held the women's all-tackle swordfish record at 772 pounds and retains the 80-pound-test record with this fish—it's heavier than the 130-pound line class record, too.

Together, the Marrons followed the other famous husband and wife fishing team of the era, the Learners, and opened the fabulous billfishing on the coast of Chile. Together, they set dozens of fishing records. Together, they hooked over 35 striped marlin on three-thread (10-pound-test) line and some 50 on six-thread. They landed eight of the former and 29 of the latter.

Together, they fished as much for science as records. So, it seems fair that their two remaining records be considered—together.

Lou Marron's All-Time, All-Tackle Record

As Mrs. Marron remembers it, Lou's all-time, all-tackle record fish came on a day fishing off their boat, the *Flying Heart*. "Lou and I built a new boat every year for the eight years or so we fished off Iquique, Chile," she said. "We'd ship it down on the Grace Line, use the boats just one year, and then donate them to Woods Hole or another oceanographic group."

The Marrons brought photographers, fisheries experts and other scientists to the area, too. They opened up new ground with the giant squid and other species they caught for medical research. Still, they had time to set records.

On the morning of May 7, 1953, the Marrons' *Flying Heart* was slowly trolling over a gentle sea off Iquique when they spotted a huge dorsal fin. This is how Mrs. Marron recounted it in her book, *Albacora*, that is still required reading for ichthyology classes at Palm Beach Atlantic College.

"'Bosco!' Lou bellowed at once.

"Everyone aboard jumped into action, and baiting began before the sound of Lou's shout had faded. Lou pulled the line off the big Fin-Nor reel and stood holding the end of the big, trailing loop in his hand. We waited, breathless. That huge dorsal fin looked like the mainsail of a windjammer.

"Eddie Wall, the veteran of many swordfish safaris, was our captain that year. With a wonderful display of skillful manipulation of boat and bait, he put that bait right across the albacora's nose. The fish turned away. Again we maneuvered. This time, with a great splash of his mighty tail, Bosco dove for the bait. 'Wham'—the sword lashed out. Lou was in the chair now, waiting and watching ... A little of the line peeled off, then a little more, faster and faster. 'Strike! Ahead with the boat,' Lou shouted. He had struck Bosco, the king of kings."

Lou Marron after dropping his bait back to the big swordfish—"albacora" to the local people—had paid out yards of line as his bait sank. The big swordfish had time to circle back, seize the bait, turn it in and swallow it before Marron set the hook. The fight raged. Twelve times Lou pumped the fish

This 1,182-pound broadbill swordfish set an IGFA all-tackle world record and also is the IGFA's 130-pound line class record. The mighty fish was caught by Lou Marron near Iquique, Chile, in 1953.

The Marrons' Marvelous Swordfish   183

to the boat with his heavy 130-pound—then called 39-thread—line. A dozen times the giant fish surged away. Then, as the huge fish reached the boat after its 13th run, Eugenie Marron took the boat's controls. Eddie Wall leaned out and grabbed the heavy leader with gloved hands. The monster thrashed. A gaff sunk home. "Bosco," the legendary monster the Marrons had sought for years was theirs.

At the dock, the fish weighed in at 1,182 pounds. It was the largest gamefish of any species caught anywhere up to that day. It had to be "Bosco," that near mythical gamefish that is the mightiest of its species.

However, as Mrs. Marron told it in her book, "Later we cut Bosco open, and soon we were probing into his body cavity ...

"'Bosco!' I shrieked at Lou, 'So you've caught Bosco, have you?' She could see it was a female.

"'All right,' he said, 'Call this one Bertha if it pleases you, but whatever you say, it is still one hell of a big fish.'"

Bosco, or Bertha, remains the largest all-tackle swordfish even more than 35 years later.

Eugenie Marron's Past And Present Records

As Eugenie Marron told it in her book, she got started fishing rather abruptly. She was perched on a piano, singing in her very best imitation of Helen Morgan, a well-known singer of the time, at a very formal party—black tie, and, in her case, black velvet long gown. Suddenly, a figure in oilskins, who "loomed impressively like a sleek seal pausing among penguins," popped in the door and stood dripping all over her rugs. In a deep, yet excited voice, he said, "The tuna are running."

Lou Marron and the other men in the party started to head for the action. As anxious fishermen have done to wives for generations, they refused to wait until Mrs. Marron could change. So she joined them, black velvet, high heels and all. By the time they reached the boat, she was soaked from the rain. She changed to an extra set of her husband's dungarees, and tried to sleep on the way offshore. It was so rough she got tossed out of her bunk below deck three times until she belted herself in place.

Just when she finally fell asleep, she was called topside. She ended up all day on deck, in the rain, running 300 pounds of dead fish through a large meat grinder to chum up a tuna. Suddenly, a big boil opened up behind the bait. It turned out to be a potential record fish that her husband Lou hooked, and with her help turning his fighting chair, played and landed. She, like the fish, was hooked! Unfortunately, Lou couldn't enter the fish for IGFA records. During the fight, a commercial fisherman had touched the line when the big tuna ran across one of his nets.

The next day Mrs. Marron was more appropriately dressed and holding the rod. She managed to crank up a 430-pound tuna—the first tuna caught by a woman off the coast of the U.S.—even though she reeled out the day with a broken rib caused by the chair's shoulder harness. It was the first of her many records, and used by New Jersey Tourism for years with the implication that, "if this little lady can catch such a big fish, just imagine what a man might do."

Mrs. Marron found that quite amusing. While she is an artist by training, only 5 feet tall and thin at that, the records she set show that, at least at lighter line tests, finesse seems as important as brute strength.

"The secret in applying light-tackle skill lies in knowing how far to go," she said, "and just when to stop." At one point, with a giant amberjack, she had her drag freeze, so she had to play the fish standing with a free spool only. Still, she boated the 38-pound amberjack in one hour and 58 minutes. She thought it was a world line test record until the line tested a few ounces heavy, and she lost another potential IGFA record. She needed even greater finesse on her then-world, all-tackle record 722-pound swordfish caught on June 7, 1954.

Eugenie Marron's Largest Swordfish

The story really started several weeks before, when on the evening of the unbelievable day that she landed five striped marlin, she fell and injured her hip and was sent to bed to heal for a couple of weeks. Big gamefishing with rods set on chair rests is mostly back and leg work. Obviously, Mrs. Marron couldn't fish. So, with this in mind, she went out and played a foul-hooked swordfish that are always more difficult to land than fair-hooked fish. Her fish was barely at the boat when the hook pulled out. The fish would have topped 700 pounds. This was on a 50-pound-test outfit usually used for striped marlin, a fish that runs half the size of a swordfish.

On the record day, the Marrons towed their usual plankton nets (on this trip they caught enough plankton to keep two Florida scientists busy for a year) and a bathythermograph designed to chart ocean temperatures. Mrs. Marron sat in the fighting chair with a 24-thread rig that ran 80-pound test.

That day her bait was a 7-pound skipjack, sewed so the hooks were well in front of the skipjack's mouth. In this way, when the swordfish grabbed and turned the bait, the hook would hold. It took five hours of boring trolling before anything happened. Then, Mrs. Marron heard her husband, Lou, say, "Those must be two fish ... Those fins are too far apart."

As the *Explorer*, their boat that record year, turned, she could see both fins belonged to a single, giant swordfish. Everybody tensed. Walt, the skipper, moved in. Lou pulled line off the reel to form the loop. Doty, the cameraman the Marrons had hired that year, crouched in the bow. Twice the fish refused the bait. The third time, the skipper, who was a bit anxious at the pressure, cut a bit too close to the lazing swordfish. The huge fish sounded and disappeared.

Then, suddenly, the fish showed again well off to port. The boat turned to follow, eased across the fish with a bit more line out and slowed. The bait passed the lazing billfish. Then, almost leisurely the two fins of the mighty fish turned. It arrowed in on the bait and slammed it with his bill. Everything stopped. The boat kicked out of gear. The loop of loose line slowly fed over the stern to give the fish time to turn and swallow the Judas bait. Eugenie Marron had her reel in freespool. They waited.

It took five minutes for the reel to tick over—then nothing. Nearly five more minutes passed. Then, gradually, faster, and faster still, the line started to move. Mrs. Marron struck with every ounce of her 110 pounds. "Boat!" she shouted as the *Explorer* shot ahead to clear line from its screws and bottom and help her set the hook.

Mrs. Marron, braced on her good leg, had locked into the lightweight side of a heavyweight fight. The big fish ran, and ran and ran. No help was possible. If anyone touched the line, the record was lost. Only as the struggle entered the second hour did the fish give, for swordfish take few prisoners. The double line eased up out of the water. Just 15 feet from the boat the fish finned, barely out of reach for the gaff. Mario, the deckhand, poised to strike home. Then, the huge fish sounded.

Inch by inch, Mrs. Marron pumped the fish up toward the boat. It was so heavy she could only gain a quarter-turn of the reel handle on each lift of the rod tip. Finally, the fish broke water 100 yards away. Mrs. Marron took the chance to relax her good leg; she could not bear much weight on her other leg because of her injured hip. As the skipper backed down on the fish, she shifted in the seat to get more back into the fight. Her feet slid off the footrest. She slammed forward. Her feet jammed under the chair's footrest. Worse, her face smashed into the big, brass reel.

Lou and the crew froze with concern; then jumped to help. "Don't touch me," she shouted, "Nobody touch me." A hand on the rod or line meant no record. So nobody moved. She slowly struggled back into position on the chair and resumed the fight. Something wasn't right. Her probing tongue felt a gap in her mouth, a pointed stump and a missing crown. Like her fish, hurt but not done, she fought on, parrying every thrust of the now-tiring swordfish.

The silver shape grudgingly moved back toward the boat. The double line came out of the water and onto the reel. The leader was almost in reach. Mrs. Marron jammed both thumbs down on the reel spool to haul the fish those last critical inches. Her husband grabbed the leader with both gloved hands. This time the gaff connected. It lacked just five minutes from two hours since the start of the struggle. Mrs. Marron's "monster" was an all-tackle record and the largest fish ever landed by a woman at the time. It still holds the 80-pound line class record. A 110-pounder with only one good leg, guts and guile landed a fish that weighed nearly 800 pounds.

Perspectives

To put Eugenie Marron's contributions in better perspective, when she started deep-sea fishing, there were, even as recently as 1935, no more than a dozen women fishing. When she wrote *Albacora* in 1957, there were more than a thousand. Today, there must be tens of thousands who followed her lead.

Long-line fishing that sets miles of lines and thousands of floats off Japanese and other ships that ravage today's oceans has radically reduced billfish populations all over the world. Swordfish seem particularly hard hit. Still, it's a big ocean. Swordfish larger than Lou Marron's record have been spotted by knowledgable observers. Captain Eddie Wall, the Marrons' skipper on the day Lou took his all-tackle record, even claimed, in a conversation just before he died, that, "Marron's fish was one of a pair. The second fish weighed 500 to 700 pounds more than the one we landed."

There are more big gamefishermen out today than ever in the past. Catch, tag and release has replaced photos—perfectly proper at the time—of dead fish hanging alongside "tired, but happy" anglers.

With a little luck, bigger swordfish could come to gaff. Kip Farrington reported a 1,565-pound fish harpooned off Chile. Still, Chilean records have given way in large part to those set off Australia in more protected waters with the help of better boats, better gear and better prepared skippers and mates than the Marrons used. Mike Leech, of the IGFA, said, "The problem off Chile is the lack of protection from the weather. You might only have a few days a month to seek swordfish far offshore."

The eventual "high tech" swordfish record won't (except those who confuse maximum weights with maximum achievement) erase either Marron's records from the memory of those who value pioneer efforts.

28

Tarpon—Champion High Jumpers

Tarpon fight fair! No other large fish offers the light-tackle fishermen such a sporting chance. Tarpon jump, where most other species sulk—deep. Tarpon cruise shallow, sandy flats, where most other big fish lurk near cover or, like offshore fish, patrol such deep water that the light-tackle fisherman can't pump them up. So, rather than look at M. Salazar's 283-pound fish taken on 30-pound-test line in Lake Maracaibo, Venezuela, on March 19, 1956, let's look at line class tarpon records set in the accessible Florida flats.

The Salazar fish seems to have disappeared. IGFA has repeatedly attempted to locate the fish and angler with no success. There seems to be no question that the record is a proper one. While Lake Maracaibo no longer produces such huge fish after its exploitation for oil, the biggest contemporary tarpon from Port Michel, Gaboon, run well over 200 pounds, and larger tarpon aren't that uncommon.

However, a better measure of fishing success may be the ratio of line test to fish weight. IGFA has 5-to-1, 10-to-1 and 20-to-1 categories for these. Bill Riesenfeld's 108-pound, 8-ounce tarpon taken on August 4, 1987, from Florida Bay, Florida, it weighed 27 times his line test!

IGFA Rigging

At first glance such records seem impossible. They are more

probable if tackle is rigged properly. "If it were not for the Bimini twist, heavy line section and shock tippet," Riesenfeld said, "you could play a fish until exhausted, and then not be able to move it in to be gaffed or released."

Even given this, there is little margin for error. The least gear failure means a lost fish and a possible lost record. "I'm meticulous about gear," he said. "Maybe it's a carryover from work (real estate investments), but you have to have everything just right."

He has several custom rods, Knightsticks, for his favorite 4-pound test, made by Jim Knight. Several outfits rigged and ready offer a quick second chance when a fish knocks a bait off or refuses one kind of lure. Riesenfeld only uses Daiwa BG15 reels, but modifies these to his taste.

"The weak spots on spinning reels are the rollers and drags," he said. "BG15 rollers are excellent, and I know how to fix the drag. Daiwa used to use a mix of Teflon and leather washers. Now they use all Teflon. I replace most of the Teflon washers with leather—I still have a small supply. Then, I use just the right amount—it's important not to use too much—of Teflon grease on the washers. This works perfectly if, but only if, you remove all tension from the washers by releasing the drags when you aren't fishing. You have to add extra lubrication more often than casual fishermen might think, as well."

Riesenfeld only uses one kind of line, too. His preferred Ande 2- and 4-pound-test seems a flats favorite with guides and other record holders like Dr. Corky Adams of bonefishing fame. "Ande seems a bit stiffer and definitely resists nicks," Riesenfeld said. "So, it stands up to the flats. I've also never had a problem with its rated tests. Some brands test too high. That can cost a world record!"

Attention to details extends to terminal tackle, too. IGFA allows 15 feet total between the end of the fisherman's "test" line and the fish. Riesenfeld says, "I tie a 4-foot Bimini twist in the end of my 4-pound-test Ande line and attach that to 10 or so feet of 30-pound-test with a short 50- and sometimes 80-pound test section at the bait or lure."

This rig allows big tarpon to jump and run without their scales or bony mouth, or mild bottom abrasion, breaking the line. Once the fish tires, the fisherman can, if his guide poles

Bill Riesenfeld is another record-holder who used the services of guide Joe Wejebe who is shown in this photo holding the 108-pound, 8-ounce tarpon taken by Riesenfeld. The fish is the IGFA men's 4-pound line class record.

Tarpon—Champion High Jumpers

strongly, move up until he plays the fish off the leader. This reduces the playing time and improves the fish's survival chances on release without giving the fisherman an unfair advantage.

Partnership On The Flats

Because tarpon, like permit and bonefish, are flats fish that live in broad, shallow bay sections off tropical coasts, fishermen usually chase these fish from a flats skiff that's powered into the area, and then worked from a platform over the raised motor by a guide using a long pole. Run motors on the flats and skittish fish scoot for deeper water!

Guides like Jose Wejebe, who led Riesenfeld to his record tarpon, find areas where records can be set with fish large enough to qualify for given line classes. Such "bathtubs" offer minimum chances for fish to go deep or hang fishermen on mangroves or other hazards.

Guides pole all day in the hot sun and Turkish bath humidity during the long search for tails, shadows or riffles that tip off working fish. Guides try to place the boat so the fisherman can see and cast to the right spot. In many cases, guides call the strike because they can see the fish pick up the bait or tap the lure where the fisherman cannot.

Once the fish is hooked, the guide must often pole hard to move in on the fish to reduce the chance of the line being caught on, and broken by bottom or floating snags or, as sometimes happens, other fish. As the fight moves into the long slogging stage that brings the fish to net or gaff, guides provide encouragement to the fisherman, keep the boat properly placed and watch out for snags. They may, without touching the line, remove floating debris, like seaweed, that collects during the fight. Then, they gaff or as is more often the case, release the fish. Finally, they need to find the way home through the often confusing, barren flats.

The fisherman needs the correct gear and, after consultation, terminal tackle. He needs to cast accurately with a quiet presentation and set the hook to the limit of his tackle. Then, he must "bow to the fish" when big tarpon jump as, when free in the water, tarpon easily snap lines. "Patience early when the fish is green and adrenalin flows fast, and concentration late as the fisherman, like his gear, tires" keys success.

As the fight enters the middle rounds, fishermen have to stay tough and keep pressure on while they try to work close and get the Bimini on the reel so they can use the leader's strength. Tension increases as the fish draws near. With less stretch due to the fight's stress and the shorter distance between fish and rodtip, the least error means a lost fish.

It's in the second and third hour that a lack of attention loses fish. When close to the boat, tarpon can do all sorts of discouraging things. Tarpon have jumped into boats—that ends it, the fish wins. The guide and fishermen spend an hour or so collecting gear from the shallow bottom if they are "lucky" enough to be over sand. Tarpon dive under boats and break lines and snag lines on motors. Only exact concentration, and a decent measure of luck, brings success with light tackle.

So flats records are really partnerships. The expectation, effort and skill each partner adds can vary widely. With experts like Riesenfeld and Wejebe, it's close to a 50-50 proposition. Both go out specifically to set new light tackle records. Riesenfeld, with Wejebe and other guides, has set single and multiple records with 4-pound test on flats species like tarpon, permit, barracuda, mutton snapper and others. His current 4-pound, test permit, a massive 44-pound, 12-ounce fish, may be the outstanding flats record of the modern era. It's bigger than the 8-pound-test record.

The Preliminaries

In the heat of record stories, it's important to realize that almost all potential record fish are lost. As Jose Wejebe tells it, "Bill Riesenfeld really worked for his record. We had some 80-pound tarpon played right to the boat and let them go because we couldn't be certain that they would be over the then-record, 76-pound fish. He came down for four years to try and get record fish.

"The year before he was on a fish for four-and-a-half hours. I must have poled nine miles. The big tarpon was close a couple of times. I got a scale off of it with a gaff. Then, it moved back into the channel, joined another school, jumped, bottomed and popped the line when it ran back through the school. I know that fish weighed about 150 pounds."

Record Recollections

Fortunately, some days things come together. Riesenfeld's record day, the second of a four-day trip, didn't start well, and it nearly came to a heartbreaking end. Jose Wejebe had his custom Dolphin Super Skiff, a hull designed on a Steve Huff pattern ready early. His favorite Mariner 90 horsepower motor with the new 3-cylinder setup was, he said, "really reliable. We run motors hard for 65 or 75 miles a day over shallows and through rough water. When you add the humidity and salt spray, it takes a tough motor and sturdy hull."

Wejebe won't disclose the exact spot he had found to fish. At the proper tide stage, it was a lovely dished flat with 3 to 4 feet of water. He had seen record tarpon there a couple of weeks before. So, with conditions perfect they were out for the record "somewhere on Florida Bay."

Their troubles started with the bait. Wejebe remembers spending a long time picking out just the right big shrimp at the tackle shop in Marathon. Shrimp are the choice flats bait, because you get a bit longer to set the hook, and a better hook set, than is the case with lures.

"When we got to the spot we wanted to fish," Wejebe said, "the bait was dead because of water conditions."

Riesenfeld said, "The aerator in the bait tank broke." These things do happen to the best of guides, and almost always at the worst of times. They could see record fish tailing everywhere. So Riesenfeld started casting with plastic worms, but rigged an alternate rod with the small-size red and white finish Bagley Finger Mullet plug.

Wejebe spotted a pod of big tarpon, but none would take a plastic worm. Riesenfeld grabbed the rod with the Finger Mullet and lead the fish with a short cast from his position on the bow. The huge silver fish rolled and as Wejebe said, "garbaged the plug."

Then, as Riesenfeld bowed to avoid a broken line, he remembers, "It jumped 7 feet in the air." The silver tarpon landed, jumped and sped off. Wejebe poled desperately. The fish jumped at least a dozen times. Both fishermen expected to see the plug come loose at any time, but it held fast throughout the fight on the Florida Bay flats.

"When I finally poled up on the fish," Wejebe said, "I

The IGFA women's 130-pound line class record is this 193-pound tarpon taken in August 1984 at South Pass, Louisiana, by Sherrlyn Marie. The men's 130-pound line class record is a 224-pound fish taken by Didier Courteau in 1985 at Port Michel, Gabon.

Tarpon—Champion High Jumpers 195

missed with the gaff. I had the wrong gaff, a heavy model, in the boat. I couldn't manage to hold the leader in one hand and set the gaff with the other."

After another run, the big tarpon moved back into range. Wejebe couldn't get the gaff in. Riesenfeld said Wejebe tried more than 30 times, but there was no way to control the leader with one hand and gaff the fish with the other. Especially after poling for miles during the two-and-a-half hour fight. Wejebe would get a shot, and the gaff would either slip off or come up with a scale as the tiring tarpon shot off in a cloud of sand.

"Then, the fish dove under the boat and around the motor," Wejebe said. "Bill jammed his rod underwater and cleared the line. We were lucky!"

Desperate to gaff the fish and with a sure record fish just out of reach, Wejebe yelled, "Bill, try to pressure him!"

Riesenfeld, unsure now that his abraded line and abused knots would hold, gently led the fish in with a long, slow lift as he took care not to snag his line on the boat. Wejebe took a deep breath, stretched as far as he could with the gaff now in both hands and jabbed the huge fish.

After a run to the nearest certified scales, the fish still weighed 108 pounds, 8 ounces. It stretched 88 inches—72 inches from the mouth to the tail's fork—and was 33 inches in girth. It beat the old record by over 30 pounds. It will be tough to beat.

29

Pacific Halibut

Taking halibut seriously would be tough if not for the fact that halibut tastes delicious. Halibut look silly. White on one side, dark on the other, these ungainly bottom-dwellers offer, depending on the viewing angle, the profiles of John Candy or Twiggy. Imagine a fish that starts like a regular species, then has one eye migrate across its head. You end up with a fish designed on the same day God made giraffes and porcupines.

Halibut records seem a bit of a joke, too. The IGFA lists Gregory C. Olsen's 356-pound, 8-ounce Pacific halibut taken from the Gastineau Channel just off Juneau, Alaska, in 1986 as the all-tackle and 30-pound line test records. It proved impossible to contact Olsen, and a number of other listed line test record holders. The most notable of these would be Gene Grimes who took a 244-pound halibut to snag the 8-pound-test record in 1988.

However, the IGFA all-tackle and line test halibut records may not even be the top dozen ever caught in Alaskan waters. Chris Batin, in his excellent book *How To Catch Alaska's Trophy Sportsfish*, notes an "Alaskan record 440-pound female caught near Point Adolphus in 1978 by Joar Savland." Recently a 450-pound halibut—the weight was estimated from a length-weight chart provided by the Pacific Halibut Commission—was landed near Chichagof Island, Alaska. None of these fish are IGFA records. Why not?

To start, there's a real problem finding certified scales of 400-plus pounds in remote Alaskan areas. Then, too, most of the really big Alaskan halibut are caught by commercial fishermen more interested in meat on the dock than sometimes arcane record requirements. One Alaska fisheries biologist said, "Sure, there are 500-pound fish around, but these are hard to come by because of increased pressures, remote areas, weather, scale problems and, most of all, the local attitude that sees halibut as cash fish."

Bang, Bang Halibut

To be brutally honest, halibut don't offer much fight for their size, once you move them off bottom. They save their efforts for the boat and, for the uninformed, the cockpit. Pulling a green halibut onboard has been described as "turning a wild bull loose in a seagoing china shop" or "about as smart as shooting yourself in the foot and then complaining because you limp." A 100-pound halibut can knock covers off hatches, trash rods and reels and, in several well-documented cases, break arms and legs. A really big halibut could crush Andre the Giant. So Alaskans shoot their halibut before they hoist them on board. This disqualifies the catch for IGFA and for most other record-gathering organizations.

Mike Leech, an IGFA spokesman at its Florida headquarters, said, "Once we allow fishermen to shoot or mutilate their catch, we throw the records open to all kinds of abuses. Shark fishermen rope whites, and tow them home without shooting them. Halibut are a lot smaller than whites."

An Alaskan fisherman, who wanted to be nameless because he didn't "want IGFA on his case" said, "Dragging big halibut home alongside a boat isn't practical in the kinds of heavy seas and with the long runs back to weighing stations we face up here. We need to get our catch onboard and iced down."

Chris Batin, an IGFA representative for Alaska, said, "I'd like to see some kind of change in the rules. Otherwise, too many outstanding catches caught in an otherwise sporting manner are disallowed."

Women's Records Larger Than Men's

One of the "outstanding catches" that did make the IGFA

This 256-pound Pacific halibut was caught in the Cook Inlet in Alaska in 1989 by angler Tim Erion.

Pacific Halibut

book is Jocelyn J. Everette's 149-pound, 8-ounce Pacific halibut from Deep Creek, Cook Inlet, Alaska. Everette's fish also qualifies for the IGFA 10-to-1 club since it came to gaff on 12-pound-test line. Mrs. Everette, an experienced fisher of big game—and also holds the women's 30-pound-test line record for Pacific blue marlin at 639 pounds said, "You can take records if you pay attention to the rules and fish where big fish are likely. Once I got the fish off bottom, it wasn't really that hard. I did get quite a bath at the boat. The water was a lot colder than Kona where we usually fish."

Perspectives

An angler willing to check the IGFA records carefully and devote some time to Alaskan halibut fishing stands a good chance of setting a record. What's important is the skill needed to tame halibut at the boat. One expert said that the best system is to slam them hard on the small of the tail. There are exposed nerves there that stun the fish. A safer method might be to add tail and gill ropes and tow the catch to the scales.

30

McReynolds' Monopoly Striper

Albert McReynolds wasn't happy, but kept casting. He, and his partner, Pat Erdman of Ventor, had spent much of the night dodging big waves on the Vermont Avenue jetty off Atlantic City, New Jersey. Days of a "Nor'easter" storm had churned up a huge surf. Howling 25-knot winds knocked the tops off 8- to 10-foot surf that crashed and boiled around the jetty. Mullet driven to shore by surging waves smashed into the rocks. Stunned, they would flutter down to the bottom or flip across the surface. This dead and dying bait attracted big stripers and the slicker-clad surf and jetty fishermen who stalk these fish from the shore. It was nearly 10 o'clock on a night better suited to Poe than piscatorial pursuits, but McReynolds kept casting.

"Some of the swells were so big," McReynolds said, "they broke over the jetty up to our knees, but conditions were just right. We knew there were bass there. We had to stay."

His buddy, Pat Erdman, already landed four stripers that, when later weighed, ran as high as 26 pounds. He also caught a bonds weakfish that nearly went to 10 pounds. Erdman wasn't bashful about slipping McReynolds a needle or three about "pilgrims" and such. Erdman's comments became more caustic after each fish. Erdman and McReynolds had cast their lures and hopes into Atlantic waters for years and they took turns with gibes and quips to pass the slow time between hits. This night Erdman had it all his way, but McReynolds kept casting.

He took what little comfort he could in the knowledge that things could be worse. At least, the wind that whipped around his ears was from his back. That beat rain and wave spume in the face, the usual pattern along the Atlantic Coast in September.

McReynolds, an employee of the Beach Patrol, and, like Erdman, a member of the West Ghost Striper and Brigantine Sportsmen's Club, really knew it wasn't his day when Erdman hooked another fish. McReynolds had spent years on and around the beach and more nights than he could remember casting off Atlantic City jetties with names familiar with Monopoly players. McReynolds seemed to face a night of "Go directly to Jail. Do not pass go. Do not collect $200."

But McReynolds kept casting as he alternately watched Erdman play his fish and the sequence of waves so he would neither cross Erdman's line nor cast into broken water. A few tails, some swirls and, every now and then, a striper, silver in the lights, punctuated the storm surge around the slick, coal-black rocks.

Then, just visible in the side of a wave barely illuminated by the faint light of the city, Erdman saw a tail, a large tail, a very large tail indeed. "Al, it's a big tail. It's a big fish," he said. Erdman was right!

McReynolds turned, braced himself, reared back and swung his Shimano 10-foot-long rod, snapping it forward. His 5½-inch-long Rebel black-back silver minnow plug sailed out on pink Ande 20-pound test propelled by the wind at his back. McReynolds tapped the spool of his Penn 710 spinning reel with his forefinger to control slack blown off by the driving wind that flattened the wave tops. The plug splashed into the water and, as McReynolds tried to bring the line tight, disappeared.

McReynolds had made his last cast for the night. It took him one hour and 40 minutes to get his plug back. One hour and 40 minutes is a long time when it's measured out in surging runs in a strong storm surf, and in careful sidesteps on a slippery, storm-battered jetty aimed at summer flounder fishermen. Most of all, it's a long time to strain back, arms, hands and wrists against an unseen fish that grew larger in McReynolds' imagination with every minute, every long run

Albert McReynolds' 78-pound, 8-ounce sea-run striped bass is the IGFA's all-tackle and 20-pound line class record holder. McReynolds caught the bass off an Atlantic City, New Jersey, seawall in 1982.

McReynolds' Monopoly Striper

and every vibration of the taut line that sang in the wind. Such imagined fish usually shrink at the net or gaff. McReynolds' did not. At least, Erdman had nothing to say except encouraging words and the offer of help.

Then, as the spent striper turned on its side and came closer, still closer, McReynolds slipped, and the striper surged. At the last minute, he almost lost the huge fish on the storm-wet jetty rocks. It lacked just 20 minutes of being midnight.

McReynolds had fished for stripers for 25 years. He had even won a major Atlantic City fishing contest. But his biggest fish scaled "only" 39 pounds. McReynolds had his fish of a lifetime, but three generations of surf casters had contributed their efforts. For surf casting didn't really start until after World War II back in the Calcutta or Burma cane pole days when Cuttyhunk linen line either burned your thumb or gave you a shower every time you cast. Back then, poles broke often enough so fishermen carried spares. Back then, lines had to be rinsed and dried after every trip. Back then, as is still true today, some of the best striped bass fishermen in the world fished the New England coast. Experts like Arnold Laine, who caught stripers by the ton with a rod and reel commercially. Or the Woolner brothers—Frank was editor for *Saltwater Sportsman*. However, none of these fishermen caught the "Big 'Un" that always lurked behind the storm-built shore break. So, their names fade. McReynolds' was to suddenly shine.

With the big fish in hand, McReynolds and Erdman scrambled back over jetty rocks, stuffed the massive striper in the car and headed for Campbell's Marine and Tackle on the Margate Bridge Causeway. The store was dark, empty. No other shops were open. So, they settled down to wait.

At 7 a.m., an employee arrived to open the store and woke Erdman and McReynolds. They hauled the huge fish in and laid it on the certified scale. Suddenly, phones rang at the local paper. Dr. Corky Campbell, who owned the shop and was both a member of the International Game Fish Association and its area record representative, rushed down to check the fish and scramble for his IGFA record book. It showed the all-tackle record for striped bass as Robert A. Rocchetta's 76-pound linesides caught off Montauk, Long Island, on July 17, 1981, that today stands as the 50-pound line class record. A check of line test records showed the 20-pound class record at 73 pounds, a monster striper caught by Anton Stetzko on Nauset Beach, Massachusetts, on November 3, 1981.

These 1981 and 1982 stripers were the remnants of early larger populations. A flush of bigger fish is almost always the signal that the fishery is in a decline. When this is coupled with the absence of juvenile fish, this sad situation seems certain.

Campbell carefully rechecked the scale. Its pointer stood at the 78-pound, 8-ounce mark. Experts later agreed that if the fish were weighed immediately, it would have run to 82 or 83 pounds. Even with the morning's shrinkage, it was clearly the world all-tackle record. Campbell measured the fish. It stretched to 53 inches and its girth was 34½ inches. Campbell explained to onlookers that he couldn't determine the fish's sex—although it was almost certainly a female—because any cut or tampering would disqualify the catch under strict the IGFA rules.

Doug Long, a New Jersey State Fisheries biologist, arrived. He estimated that the huge fish—it was later determined to be indeed a female—was between 30 and 40 years old. The fish, carefully iced by Campbell, was sent to Florida for mounting. It's nice to know that a striper born perhaps during World War II, could evade a generation of fishermen, miles of nets, and the huge volume of pollution that so heavily impacted the East Coast during this period.

McReynolds had caught a unique fish, one that later, after a certain amount of confusion and conflict, earned him $100,000 from Garcia for breaking the world record. He had, moreover, caught it on 20-pound-test line. This didn't sit particularly well with some of the surf fraternity, and there were considerable rumors about the fish and where and how it was caught. This didn't seem to sit particularly well with McReynolds who took his winnings and went to Hawaii where he has apparently dropped out of sight.

IGFA investigated the catch carefully; so did others. Nobody could prove the rumored problems with the catch, although some tried. McReynolds' record stood up.

Appendix

International Game Fish Association

The following international angling rules have been formulated by the International Game Fish Association to promote ethical and sporting angling practices, to establish uniform regulations for the compilation of world game fish records, and to provide basic angling guidelines for use in fishing tournaments and any other group-angling activities.

The word *angling* is defined as catching or attempting to catch fish with a rod, reel, line and hook as outlined in the international angling rules. There are some aspects of angling that cannot be controlled through rulemaking, however. Angling regulations cannot insure an outstanding performance from each fish, and world records cannot indicate the amount of difficulty in catching the fish. Captures in which the fish has not fought or has not had a chance to fight do not reflect credit on the fisherman, and only the angler can properly evaluate the degree of achievement in establishing the record.

Only fish caught in accordance with IGFA international angling rules, and within the intent of these rules, will be considered for world records by the IGFA.

Following are the rules for freshwater and saltwater fishing. (Separate rules govern fly fishing records and should be obtained from IGFA headquarters.)

Rules For Fishing In Fresh- And Saltwater

Equipment Regulations

A. Line
1. Monofilament, multifilament and lead core multifilament lines may be used. For line classes see *World Record Requirements*.
2. Wire lines are prohibited.

B. Line Backing

1. Backing not attached to the fishing line is permissible with no restrictions as to size or material.

2. If the fishing line is attached to the backing, the catch shall be classified under the heavier of the two lines. The backing may not exceed the 130 lb (60 kg) line class and must be of a type of line approved for use in these angling rules.

C. Double Line

The use of a double line is not required. If one is used, it must meet the following specifications:

1. A double line must consist of the actual line used to catch the fish.

2. Double lines are measured from the start of the knot, braid, roll or splice making the double to the farthermost end of the knot, splice, snap, swivel or other device used for securing the trace, leader, lure or hook to the double line.

Saltwater species: In all line classes up to and including 20 lb (10 kg), the double line shall be limited to 15 feet (4.57 meters). The combined length of the double line and leader shall not exceed 20 feet (6.1 meters).

The double line on all classes of tackle over 20 lb (10 kg) shall be limited to 30 feet (9.14 meters). Combined length of double line and leader shall not exceed 40 feet (12.19 meters).

Freshwater species: The double line on all classes of tackle shall not exceed 6 feet (1.82 meters). The combined length of the double line and the leader shall not exceed 10 feet (3.04 meters).

D. Leader

The use of a leader is not required. If one is used, it must meet the following specifications:

1. The length of the leader is the overall length including any lure, hook arrangement or other device. The leader must be connected to the line with a snap, knot, splice, swivel or other device. Holding devices are prohibited. There are no regulations regarding the material or strength of the leader.

Saltwater species: In all line classes up to and including 20 lb (10 kg), the leader shall be limited to 15 feet (4.57 meters). The combined length of the double line and leader shall not exceed 20 feet (6.1 meters).

The leader on all classes of tackle over 20 lb (10 kg) shall be limited to 30 feet (9.14 meters). The combined length of the double line and leader shall be limited to 40 feet (12.19 meters).

Freshwater species: The leader on all classes of tackle shall be limited to 6 feet (1.82 meters). The combined length of the double line and leader shall not exceed 10 feet (3.04 meters).

E. Rod

1. Rods must comply with sporting ethics and customs. Considerable latitude is allowed in the choice of a rod, but rods giving the angler an unfair advantage will be disqualified. This rule is intended to eliminate the use of unconventional rods.

2. The rodtip must be a minimum of 40 inches (101.6 cm) in length. The rod butt cannot exceed 27 inches (68.58 cm) in length. These measurements must be made from a point directly beneath the center of the reel. A curved butt is measured in a straight line. (The above measurements do not apply to surf casting rods.)

Appendix

F. Reel

1. Reels must comply with sporting ethics and customs.

2. Power driven reels of any kind are prohibited. This includes motor, hydraulic or electrically driven reels and any device which gives the angler an unfair advantage.

3. Ratchet handle reels are prohibited.

4. Reels designed to be cranked with both hands at the same time are prohibited.

G. Hooks For Baitfishing

1. For live or dead baitfishing no more than two single hooks may be used. Both must be firmly imbedded in or securely attached to the bait. The eyes of the hooks must be no less than a hook's length (the length of the largest hook used) apart and no more than 18 inches (45.72 cm) apart. The only exception is that the point of one hook may be passed through the eye of the other hook.

2. The use of a dangling or swinging hook is prohibited. Double or treble hooks are prohibited.

3. A two-hook rig for bottom fishing is acceptable if it consists of two single hooks on separate leaders or drops. Both hooks must be imbedded in the respective baits and separated sufficiently so that a fish caught on one hook cannot be foul-hooked by the other.

4. All record applications made for fish caught on two-hook tackle must be accompanied by a photograph or sketch of the hook arrangement.

H. Hooks And Lures

1. When using an artificial lure with a skirt or trailing material, no more than two single hooks may be attached to the line, leader or trace. The hooks need not be attached separately. The eyes of the hooks must be no less than an overall hook's length (the overall length of the largest hook used) apart and no more than 12 inches (30.48 cm) apart. The only exception is that the point of one hook may be passed through the eye of the other hook. The trailing hook may not extend more than a hook's length beyond the skirt of the lure. A photograph or sketch showing the hook arrangement must accompany a record application.

2. Gang hooks are permitted when attached to plugs and other artificial lures that are specifically designed for this use. Gang hooks must be free swinging and shall be limited to a maximum of three hooks (either single, double, or treble or a combination of any three). Baits may not be used with gang hooks. A photograph or sketch of the plug or lure must be submitted with record applications.

I. Other Equipment

1. *Fighting chairs* may not have any mechanically propelled devices which aid the angler in fighting a fish.

2. *Gimbals* must be free swinging, which includes gimbals that swing in a vertical plane only. Any gimbal that allows the angler to reduce strain or to rest while fighting the fish is prohibited.

3. *Gaffs and nets* used to boat or land a fish must not exceed 8 feet (2.49 meters) in overall length. In using a flying or detachable gaff, the rope may not exceed 30 feet (9.14 meters). The gaff rope must be measured from the point where it is secured to the detachable head to the other end. Only the effective length will be considered. If a fixed head gaff is used, the same limitations shall apply and the gaff rope shall be measured from the same location on the gaff

hook. Only a single hook is permitted on any gaff. Harpoon or lance attachments are prohibited. Tail ropes are limited to 30 feet (9.14 meters). (When fishing from a bridge, pier, or other high platform or structure, this length limitation does not apply.)

4. *Floats* are prohibited with the exception of any small flotation device attached to the line or leader for the sole purpose of regulating the depth of the bait. The flotation device must not in any way hamper the fighting ability of the fish.

5. *Entangling devices*, either with or without a hook, are prohibited and may not be used for any purpose including baiting, hooking, fighting or landing the fish.

6. *Outriggers, downriggers and kites* are permitted to be used provided that the actual fishing line is attached to the snap or other release device, either directly or with some other material. The leader or double line may not be connected to the release mechanism either directly or with the use of a connecting device.

7. A *safety line* may be attached to the rod provided that it does not in any way assist the angler in fighting the fish.

Angling Regulations

1. From the time that a fish strikes or takes a bait or lure, the angler must hook, fight and land or boat the fish without the aid of any other person, except as provided in these regulations.

2. If a rod holder is used and a fish strikes or takes the bait or lure, the angler must remove the rod from the holder as quickly as possible. The intent of this rule is that the angler shall strike and hook the fish with the rod in hand.

3. In the event of a multiple strike on separate lines being fished by a single angler, only the first fish fought by the angler will be considered for a world record.

4. If a double line is used, the intent of the regulations is that the fish will be fought on the single line most of the time that it takes to land the fish.

5. A harness may be attached to the reel or rod, but not to the fighting chair. The harness may be replaced or adjusted by a person other than the angler.

6. Use of a rod belt or waist gimbal is permitted.

7. When angling from a boat, once the leader is brought within the grasp of the mate, or the end of the leader is wound to the rodtip, more than one person is permitted to hold the leader.

8. One or more gaffers may be used in addition to persons holding the leader. The gaff handle must be in hand when the fish is gaffed.

9. The angling and equipment regulations shall apply until the fish is weighed.

The Following Acts Will Disqualify A Catch:

1. Failure to comply with equipment or angling regulations.

2. The act of persons other than the angler in touching any part of the rod, reel or line (including the double line) either bodily or with any device, from the time a fish strikes or takes the bait or lure, until the fish is either landed or released, or in giving any aid other than that allowed in the rules and regulations. If an obstacle to the passage of the line through the rod guides has to be removed from the line, then the obstacle (whether chum, floatline, rubber band or other material) shall be held and cut free. Under no circumstances should the line be held or touched by anyone other than the angler during this process.

3. Resting the rod in a rod holder, on the gunwale of the boat, or any other object while playing the fish.

4. Handling or using a handline or rope attached in any manner to the angler's line or leader

Appendix

for the purpose of holding or lifting the fish.

5. Shooting, harpooning or lancing any fish (including sharks and halibuts) at any stage of the catch.

6. Chumming with or using as bait the flesh, blood, skin or any part of mammals other than hair or pork rind used in lures designed for trolling or casting.

7. Using a boat or device to beach or drive a fish into shallow water in order to deprive the fish of its normal ability to swim.

8. Changing the rod or reel while the fish is being played.

9. Splicing, removing or adding to the line while the fish is being played.

10. Intentionally foul-hooking a fish.

11. Catching a fish in a manner that the double line never leaves the rodtip.

12. Using a size or kind of bait that is illegal to possess.

13. Attaching the angler's line or leader to part of a boat or other object for the purpose of holding or lifting the fish.

14. If a fish escapes before gaffing or netting and is recaptured by any method other than as outlined in the angling rules.

The Following Situations Will Disqualify A Catch:

1. When a rod breaks (while the fish is being played) in a manner that reduces the length of the tip below minimum dimensions or severely impairs its angling characteristics.

2. Mutilation to the fish, prior to landing or boating the catch, caused by sharks, other fish, mammals or propellers that remove or penetrate the flesh. (Injuries caused by leader or line, scratches, old healed scars or regeneration deformities are not considered to be disqualifying injuries.) Any mutilation on the fish must be shown in a photograph and fully explained in a separate report accompanying the record application.

3. When a fish is hooked or entangled on more than one line.

Regulations Governing Record Catches

General Information

1. Protested applications or disputed existing records will be referred to the IGFA Executive Committee for review. Its decisions will be final. IGFA reserves the right to refuse to consider an application or grant a claim for a record or fishing contest application. All IGFA decisions will be based upon the intent of the regulations.

2. When a substantial award is specifically offered for a world record catch in any line or tippet class, only a claim for an all-tackle record will be considered.

3. In some instances, an IGFA officer or member of the International Committee or a deputy from a local IGFA member club may be asked to recheck information supplied on a claim. Such action is not to be regarded as doubt of the formal affidavit, but rather as evidence of the extreme care with which IGFA investigates and maintains its records.

Species Identification

1. Photographs must be submitted by which positive identification of the exact species can be made. Read the rules on photographs at the end of this section, and refer to the Species Identification section in the *World Record Game Fishes* book to determine which features must show to identify your fish. Applications without photographs will not be accepted.

2. If there is the slightest doubt that the fish cannot be properly identified from the photographs and other data submitted, the fish should be examined by an ichthyologist or qualified fishery biologist before a record or contest application is submitted to IGFA. The scientist's signature and title (or qualifications) should appear on the IGFA application form or on a separate document confirming the identification of the species.

3. If a scientist is not available, the fish should be retained in a preserved or frozen condition until a qualified authority can verify the species or until notified by IGFA that the fish need no longer be retained.

4. If no decision can be made from the photographs and the angler can provide no further proof of the identification of the species, the record claim will not be considered.

Witnesses To Catch

On all record claims, witnesses to the catch are highly desirable if at all possible. Unwitnessed catches may be disallowed if questions arise regarding their authenticity. It is important that the witnesses can attest to the angler's compliance with the IGFA International Angling Rules and Equipment Regulations.

Minimum Weight Requirements For Vacant Records

1. The minimum acceptance weight for any record catch claim is 1 pound (.453 kg).

2. Minimum acceptance weights have been established for many of the vacant record categories. Anglers should check the record listings for minimum weight requirements before submitting a record claim.

Weights Needed To Defeat Or Tie Existing Records

1. To replace a record for a fish weighing less than 25 pounds (11.33 kg), the replacement must weigh at least 2 ounces (56.69 gm) more than the existing record.

2. To replace a record for a fish weighing 25 pounds (11.33 kg) or more, the replacement must weigh at least one half of 1 percent more than the existing record. *Examples:* At 100 pounds (45.35 kg) the additional weight required would be 8 ounces (226.7 gm); at 200 pounds (90.71 kg) the additional weight required would be 1 pound (.45 kg).

3. Any catch which matches the weight of an existing record or exceeds the weight by less than the amount required to defeat the record will be considered a tie. In case of a tie claim involving more than two catches, weight must be compared with the original record (first fish to be caught). Nothing weighing less than the original record will be considered.

4. Estimated weights will not be accepted. (See *Weighing Requirements.*) Fractions of ounces of their metric equivalents will not be considered.

Time Limit On Claims

With the exception of *all-tackle records* only, claims for record fish caught in U.S. continental waters must be received by IGFA within 60 days of the date of catch. Claims for record fish caught in other waters must be received by IGFA within three months of the date of catch.

Claims for all-tackle records only are considered for catches made in past years if (1) acceptable photographs are submitted, (2) the weight of the fish can be positively verified, and (3) the method of catch can be substantiated. For catches made in the past, as much information as possible must be submitted on an IGFA world record application form with any

Appendix

additional substantiating data.

If an incomplete record claim is submitted, it must be accompanied by an explanation of why certain portions are incomplete. An incomplete claim will be considered for a record if the following conditions are met:

1. The incomplete claim with explanations of why portions are incomplete must be received by IGFA within the time limits specified above.

2. Missing data must be due to circumstances beyond the control of the angler making the record claim.

3. All missing data must be supplied within a period of time considered to be reasonable in view of the particular circumstances.

Final decisions on incomplete claims will be made by IGFA's Executive Committee.

Weighing Requirements For Record Fish

1. The fish must be weighed by an official weighmaster (if one is available) or by an IGFA official or by a recognized local person familiar with the scale. Disinterested witnesses to the weight should be used whenever possible.

2. The weight of the sling, platform or rope (if one is used to secure the fish on the scales) must be determined and deducted from the total weight.

3. At the time of weighing, the actual tackle used by the angler to catch the fish must be exhibited to the weighmaster and weight witness.

4. No estimated weights will be accepted. Fish weighed only at sea or on other bodies of water will not be accepted.

5. Only weights indicated by the graduations on the scale will be accepted. Visual frationalizing of these graduations is not allowed. Any weights that fall between two graduations on the scale must be rounded to the lower of the two.

6. All record fish should be weighed on scales that have been checked and certified for accuracy by government agencies or other qualified and accredited organizations. All scales must be regularly checked for accuracy and certified in accordance with applicable government regulations at least once every 12 months. If at the time of weighing the fish, the scale had not been properly certified within 12 months, it should be checked and certified for accuracy as quickly as possible, and an official report stating the findings of the inspection prior to any adjustment of the scale must be included with the record application.

7. If there is no official government inspector or accredited commercial scales representative available in the area where the fish is weighed, the scales must be checked by weighing objects of recognized and proven weight. Objects weighed must be at least equal to the weight of the fish. Substantiation of the correct weight of these objects must be submitted to IGFA along with the names and complete addresses of accredited witnesses to the entire procedure.

8. In extremely remote areas where no weighing scales are available, it will be permissible for the angler to use his own scales providing that they are of a quality type and have been properly certified both before and after returning from the fishing trip.

9. IGFA reserves the right to require any scale to be recertified for accuracy if there are any indications that the scale might not have weighed correctly.

Preparation Of Record Claims

To apply for a world record, the angler must submit a completed IGFA application form, the mandatory length of line and terminal tackle (described below) used to catch the fish, and acceptable photographs of the fish, the tackle used to catch the fish, the scale used to weigh the fish and the angler with the fish.

Application Form

The official IGFA world record application form or a reproduction must be used for record claims. This form may be reproduced as long as all items are included.

The angler must fill in the application personally. IGFA also recommends that the angler personally mail the application, line sample or fly leader and photographs.

When making any record claim, the angler must indicate the specified strength of the line or tippet used to catch the fish. In the cases of line class and tippet class records, this will place the claim in an IGFA line or tippet class category (see *World Class Categories*). All lines will be examined by IGFA to verify the specified strength of the line. If the line or tippet overtests its particular category, the application will be considered in the next highest category; if it undertests into a lower line or tippet class category, the application will not be considered for the lower line class. The heaviest line class permitted for both freshwater and saltwater records is 60 kg (130 lb) class. The heaviest tippet class permitted for fly fishing records is 8 kg (16 lb). If the line or tippet overtests these maximum strengths, the claim will be disallowed.

Extreme care should be exercised in measuring the fish as the measurements are often important for weight verification and scientific studies. See the measurement diagram on the record application to be sure you have measured correctly.

The angler is responsible for seeing that the necessary signatures and correct addresses of the boat captain, weighmaster and witnesses are on the application. If an IGFA officer or representative, or an officer or member of an IGFA club is available, he or she should be asked to witness the claim. The name of a boatman, guide or weighmaster repeated as witness is not acceptable.

The angler must appear in person to have his application notarized. In territories where notarization is not possible or customary, the signature of a government commissioner or resident, a member of an embassy, legation or consular staff or an IGFA officer or International Committee member may replace notarization.

Any deliberate falsification of an application will disqualify the applicant for any future IGFA world record, and any existing records will be nullified.

Line Sample

All applications for freshwater and saltwater line class records must be accompanied by the entire leader, the double line and at least 50 feet (15.24 meters) of the single line closest to the double line, leader or hook. All line samples and the leader (if one is used) must be submitted in one piece. If a lure is used with the leader, the leader should be cut at the eye attachment to the lure.

Each line sample must be in one piece. It must be submitted in a manner that it can be easily unwound without damage to the line. A recommended method is to take a rectangular piece of stiff cardboard and cut notches in two opposite ends. Secure one end of the line to the cardboard and wind the line around the cardboard through the notched areas. Secure the other end, and write your name and the specified strength of the line on the cardboard. Any line sample submitted that is tangled or cannot be easily unwound will not be accepted.

Appendix 213

Photographs

Photographs showing the full length of the fish, the rod and reel used to make the catch, and the scale used to weigh the fish must accompany each record application. A photograph of the angler with the fish is also required.

So that there can be no question of species identification, the clearest possible photos should be submitted. This is especially important in the cases of hybrids and fishes that may be confused with similar species. Shark applications should include a photograph of the shark's teeth, and of the head and back taken from above in addition to the photographs taken from the side. Whether the shark has or does not have a ridge between the dorsal fins should be clearly evident in this photograph.

In all cases, photographs should be taken of the fish in a hanging position and also lying on a flat surface on its side. The fish should be broadside to the camera and no part of the fish should be obscured. The fins must be fully extended and not obscured with the hands, and the jaw or bill clearly shown. Avoid obscuring the keels of sharks and tunas with a tail rope.

When photographing a fish lying on its side, the surface beneath the fish should be smooth and a ruler or marked tape placed beside the fish if possible. Photographs from various anglers are most helpful.

An additional photograph of the fish on the scale with actual weight visible helps to expedite the application.

Photos taken by daylight with a reproducible-type negative film are highly recommended if at all possible.

Note: IGFA's bimonthly newsletter The International Angler keeps anglers up to date on world record catches. It is important that IGFA have clear, publishable photographs of the fish and the angler. If you have action shots of the catch, IGFA would like to see them also.

(Reprinted with permission from the International Game Fish Association)

National Fresh Water Fishing Hall Of Fame:

Tips On Establishing A Record Catch

When you suspect you have a fish on your line which is large for its species and may be a record catch, do not allow another person to touch your line or tackle during the encounter. More than one person involved in subduing the fish may disqualify the catch (except for help in netting or gaffing).

Get the fish to a certified or balance type scale (one legal for trade) as soon as possible. Such scales are found in stores, post offices, fisheries, medical facilities, industry, feed mills, and often in sport shops, tourism centers or resorts.

To insure unquestionable accuracy, us a scale to which is affixed a seal bearing a number, inspector and date of check. Spring mechanism type scales are sometimes inaccurate, but may be used if they can later be verified for accuracy in case you are in a place where a certified scale is not available. Such spring scale check/verification documents would then be required to be submitted.

Weigh your fish ONLY ONCE in the presence of two disinterested witnesses and get their full names and addresses. Measure girth, fork length and total length.

Have your fish identified as to species by a professional fisheries person or taxonomist. If the fish is a suspected hybrid or a potential all-tackle record, have its species identified by a CERTIFIED fish biologist or taxonomist. Get such identifier's full name, address and place of employment.

Have photos taken. Color is best. Hold fish broadside for further positive identification purposes. If possible, take a black and white picture also for future press reprint purpose. Use a good camera, take a well-lighted, clear, sharp, close-up photo. For small fish close-ups, waist shots are best.

Do not open the fish. This may be required later in the presence of witnesses to verify weight if suspicion arises. Meanwhile, keep the catch cold-fresh or frozen until status is determined. A taxidermist can mount a fish that has been frozen.

Save the first 25 feet or more of line next to the hook/bait to later send with your application for laboratory line test purpose. Wind line on notched cardboard to avoid kinks or tangles. For fly fishing records, save 15 inches or more of the tippet used, leaving the fly/hook attached. For rod/line/no reel, or ice fishing records, only heaviest of species is recognized, so a line sample need not be submitted.

For world record application and rules form, write or call the National Fresh Water Fishing Hall of Fame, Box 33, Hall of Fame Drive, Hayward, Wisconsin 54843, phone (715) 634-4440.

For local record application contact the state or providence DNR or Fish and Game Commission. All the above services are free as a public service.

Rules For National Fresh Water Hall of Fame Records

Definitions For Eligibility:

Division #1 — Rod/Reel

The use of a fixed or revolving spool affixed to a fishing rod both which are carriers of line to which are affixed legal single or multiple hooks by which the fish is captured. All-Tackle (heaviest) and line classes recognized. Submit 25 feet or more of line sample used in the catch.

Division #2 — Fly Fishing

The use of regulation fly fishing equipment cast to the prey in conventional fly fishing manner. All-Tackle (heaviest) and line classes recognized. Submit 15 inches of tippet with fly/hook attached. Fly/hook returned on request. (Note: Hybrid equipment not allowed.)

Division #3 — Pole/Line/No Reel

The use of a pole and line without a reel for retrieve purpose. (Ice fishing excluded, see Division #4.) Only heaviest catches recognized. No line sample needed.

Division #4 — Ice Fishing

A fish captured through the ice by accepted legal ice fishing devices such as a pole/line, tip-up and other varied legal devices. Only heaviest catches recognized. No line sample needed.

Division #5 — Miscellaneous Methods

The legal capture of fish by methods other than defined in the first four divisions an only those species or methods listed by the Fishing Hall of Fame is its book of records. Currently, only the five heaviest Paddlefish catches are recognized in this division. No line sample needed.

Eligible Waters

Any world fresh water except private, club or fish hatchery waters or private ponds not accessible for angling by the general public. Fee waters and ponds for angling by permit to public allowed. Inquire.

Species Recognized For World Records ... Minimum Weights

Any sport caught fish species will be recognized that meets rules requirements. Species not currently listed because of no demand will be added if demand dictates.

Fish catches less than one (1) pound will not be considered. Weights may be certified in pounds and ounces or metric. One (1) ounce graduations recognized for record purposes. Fractions discounted.

Legal Season ... Legal Catch

Fish must be taken legally during legal season and hours for the specific geographic location.

More than one person involved in subduing the fish may disqualify the catch (except for help in netting or gaffing).

The Rod/Pole

Hall of Fame world line class or all tackle records are recognized only when a rod/pole (minimum 36" open water conventional angling; minimum 18" ice fishing; minimum 72" fly fishing lengths) to which a line and bait are attached is used.

Hand lines, jig boards, spears, snag-hooks, trot lines, gill nets, set lines, or stub line carriers, etc., will not be considered.

The only exception to the rod/pole regulation is the use of a tip-up for ice fishing, whose catch may be a contender for only the "heaviest" in Ice Fishing, Division #4, and methods allowed in miscellaneous Division #5 for heaviest in that division.

The Reel

Power driven reels (motor/electric) are prohibited.

The Bait

The word "bait" as used here is that portion of tackle which entices the fish to bite whether live, plug, lure, fly, etc.

All Tackle (Heaviest) Class

Heaviest fish caught of the species regardless of line test used. Only rod/bait catches eligible.

Line Class Classification

The heaviest fish caught of the species on a line test or strength. These classes are recognized: Division #1 — 2 lb., 4 lb., 6 lb., 8 lb., 10 lb., 12 lb., 14 lb., 15 lb., 16 lb., 17 lb., 20 lb., 25 lb., 30 lb., 36 lb., 40 lb., 45 lb., 50 lb., 60 lb., 70 lb., 80 lb., 130 lb., and Unlimited. Division #2 — Tippets 2 lb., 4 lb., 6 lb., 8 lb., 10 lb., 12 lb., 14 lb., 16 lb., and Unlimited.

A range of line classes have been determined for each listed species. Fish caught on line classes beyond the listed range for that species are placed in a record class defined as "Unlimited." Example: Panfish may have a recognition class from 2 lb. test to 12 lb. test, while larger species class recognition may culminate in heavier maximum line strengths.

Line Testing Procedure: Division #1 — Rod/Reel

The first 25 feet or more of the line used in the catch MUST be submitted with the application for Division #1 — Rod/Reel. Five tests are made of each line to average breaking load. *Example:* A line may test stronger or weaker than its stated strength due to many variables. To accommodate this, parameters are used.

Example: A six (6) lb. test line parameter is from 5.01 to 7.00. An average breaking point below would place that line in the 4 lb. class while an average breaking load above would place that line in the 8 lb. class, etc. Each qualifying applicant receives a detailed lab copy of his line's test results. Our lab uses only certified line test equipment. Line tested wet strength.

Line Testing Procedure: Division #2 — Fly Fishing

Submit tippet with fly/hook attached. Fly/hook will be returned on request. Because of the shortness of the tippet only a single break load test is possible. The .01 to .00 parameter for test is used as in Division #1.

Pole/Line/No Reel ... Ice Fishing ... Miscellaneous Divisions

Do not submit line samples for these divisions. *Only* heaviest recognized; *no* line classes.

Applicant's Agreement

In submitting this application, the applicant agrees to allow the Hall of Fame to use record photos and stated facts for publication as it sees fit.

Do Not Open Fish If "All Tackle"

Before status is determined. This may be required by a biologist to authenticate weight.

Appendix

Weigh-In On Legal-For-Trade Scale

Weigh your potential record *only once* one a certified/balance-type scale *legal for trade* which carries a certification, inspection and date or sliding weight and balance type scales. Do not use a spring-type scale unless it has been, or can be, certified for accuracy by quality or later proper authority. Certified scales are found in stores, post offices, feed mills, industry, etc. While witnesses to catch are desirable but not mandatory, two disinterested witnesses to weight are *positively* required. (The applicant cannot be a witness.)

Species Identification

A *professional fisheries person* MUST identify your catch as to species and attest to the correct identity. If all-tackle record or hybrid, a taxonomist or DNR fish biologist is required.

Send In Line Sample

Division #1 — Rod/Reel — Submit at least the first 25 feet of line used in the catch wound on notched stiff cardboard to prevent tangles or kinks. Line tested wet strength. Do not use tape on line. Division #2 — Fly Fishing — Submit tippet (15 inches) or more with fly/hook attached. Fly/hook returned on request. Line tested wet strength. Do not use tape on line.

Send In Photos

A *good* colored photo of the angler and the fish (taken broadside for further identification) MUST be submitted. This photo will ultimately be displayed in the Hall's museum records gallery. Also, submit two (2) or more good black and white photos of you and the fish (broadside), for news and publicity purposes (not mandatory). Fish should predominate in all photos, *not* the angler. For small fish, waist shots are best.

Notary Public Attest

All applications *must* be notarized as provided on the form.

The Application

Do not submit unless complete. Please print information (PLAINLY), especially your full name and correct address. You're on your sportsman's honor. Misrepresentation or falsifying an application with intent to defraud the program will disqualify the catch and create suspect of past or future catches. Applications lacking the vital requirements as determined by the qualifier will be returned or rejected. Application must be received within 90 days of catch. Exceptions will be allowed for good reason only as determined by the qualifier. Properly documented dated records can be considered.

The National Fresh Water Fishing Hall of Fame reserves the sole right to grant or reject any record, past or future, for good reason which it has listed or established. Its decision is final.

Qualifier's Options

The qualifier reserves the right to suspect, review, investigate, reject, disqualify or accept any declaration of record submitted, or any record inadvertently granted. In cases of dispute, the Hall's "Records Board of Review" shall be the final authority. In submitting application, the angler voluntary submits to these options of the qualifier.

Complete Angler's Library